Test Prep and Admissions

101
Ways to Become
the Perfect
College Applicant

by Jeanine Le Ny and the Kaplan Admissions Team

Simon & Schuster

NEW YORK · LONDON · SYDNEY · TORONTO

Kaplan Publishing
Published by SIMON & SCHUSTER
Rockefeller Center
1230 Avenue of the Americas
New York, NY 10020

Several tips in this book adapted from Kaplan Admissions Modules 1-6 © 2005, Kaplan, Inc.

Tip #21 adapted from "Where Does Time Go," from Cook Counseling Center at Virginia Polytechnic Institute and State University (ucc.vt.edu/stdysk/TMInteractive.html).

Editorial Director: Jennifer Farthing
Project Editor: Megan Gilbert
Production Manager: Michael Shevlin
Content Manager: Patrick Kennedy
Interior Design and Page Layout: Dave Chipps
Cover Design: Mark Weaver

Manufactured in the United States of America.
Published simultaneously in Canada.

10 9 8 7 6 5 4 3 2 1

October 2005

ISBN-13: 978-0-7432-7875-1
ISBN-10:   0-7432-7875-5

For information regarding special discounts for bulk purchases, please contact Simon & Schuster Special Sales at 1-800-456-6798 or business@simonandschuster.com.

Introduction

There's no doubt that the college admissions process is more stressful than ever. Not only do you need to be at the top of your game grade-wise, these days you've got to "make your mark" in high school, too. You probably have tons of people telling you that you HAVE to be captain of the football team, student-body president, a concert pianist, AND solve the problem of world hunger just to get NOTICED by a top college . . . all while holding down a part-time job at the mall. Oh, and don't forget those perfect SAT and ACT scores!

Seems impossible, right?

Well, **Kaplan** is here to make it a little easier on you. **101 Ways to Become the Perfect College Applicant** gives you the INSIDER'S SCOOP from Kaplan Admissions experts on what it takes to get competitive without going crazy!

- Need to know how many extracurricular activities you should be involved with **in order to stand out**? Turn to the "Ways to Make Yourself a Good Candidate" section.

- Don't know the first thing about a college fair or even what to look for in a school? Check out the "Steps to Choosing the Right College for You" section.

- Find tips on how to handle parental pressure in the "Helpful Relationships" section.

- Learn the insider's route to recommendations, financial aid, and more in the "Steps to the Perfect Application" section.

- Get great advice on everything from roommates to time management in the "Ten Things to Remember Once You Get In" section.

If that's not enough, the Kaplan Admissions Team can also offer you loads of personalized advice when it comes to planning for college, researching schools, developing memorable essays, and preparing winning applications that will help you get accepted into the college of your choice. Call **1-800-KAP-TEST** or visit **kaptest.com/collegeadmissions** to find out how you can work with our nationwide network of consultants.

And remember, you don't have to drive yourself nuts being a superhuman student—not when you've got the insider's tools to become the perfect college applicant.

Good luck!

About the Authors

Jeanine Le Ny has created and edited dozens of best-selling novels for teens and young readers, and has recently become a full-time author. She resides in New York City with her husband, and enrolls in college classes every chance she gets.

Kathleen Martin is a senior Kaplan College Admissions Consultant with more than 17 years of college admissions experience. Throughout her career, she has reviewed more than 10,000 applications, read an equal number of student essays, and performed thousands of admissions interviews. As a consultant, she has successfully guided hundreds of families through the college admissions process. Kathleen is particularly familiar with top-tier liberal arts schools, and has helped students gain admission to Georgetown, Cornell, Williams, Boston University, and Indiana University, among others. She also has experience working with transfer students, prep school students, learning-disabled students, and physically challenged students. After earning her undergraduate degree in speech communications, psychology, and sociology from Ithaca College, Kathleen served as the Senior Associate Director of Admissions at Moravian College.

Stephen O'Leary is a Kaplan College Admissions Consultant, with over 28 years of experience in college counseling. He was Director of Guidance for the Marblehead and Somerville, Massachusetts school systems as well as Director of Student Services for the Groton-Dunstable Regional School District in Groton, Massachusetts. For the past 20 years, Steve has trained career and college counselors as an adjunct professor in the masters-level counseling programs at Salem State College and Fitchburg State College in Massachusetts. Steve has extensive experience working with students who are interested in Ivy League colleges, strong liberal arts colleges, collegiate athletic programs, and appropriate four-year programs for students with learning disabilities. In addition to his membership in the National Association for College Admission Counseling, Steve is a member of the Massachusetts School Counselors' Association.

Part One:

Ways to Make Yourself a Good Candidate

1

Start thinking about your plans as early as possible.

It's never too soon to start down the road to college. We know what you're thinking—you've got to get used to a new school, make new friends and meet new teachers, **AND** think about college too? You don't know what you want to eat for lunch let alone where you want to be after you graduate or what you have to do to get there! Don't worry—we're here to help. Keep reading!

Keep your options open

As a freshman, you don't have to know **EXACTLY** where you want to go to college, but it's a good idea to decide what **TYPE** of college you want to attend—then gear your high school classes toward the requirements.

DON'T FREAK OUT!

Here's what most highly competitive colleges and universities want to see on your transcript:

- Four years of English
- Four years of Math
- Four years of Science
- Four years of Social Studies
- Three years of a single Foreign Language
- Two years of Fine Arts or Performing Arts
- One year (or more) of Computers

Don't just dream it— achieve it!

Get with a plan, man!

High school is a busy time, and you need to get organized if you want to get through it in one piece. There's nothing like making a list to make you feel like you know what you're doing as you prepare for college. Here are some ideas to get you started:

Freshman Year

- Develop good study skills, and set goals for high grades.
- Try out interesting extracurricular activities.
- Form relationships with your favorite teachers.

Sophomore Year

- Maintain good grades.
- Commit to your favorite extracurricular activities.
- Take PSAT practice tests.
- Take the SAT Subject Test for courses recently completed, such as Biology.
- Do something over the summer to further your interests.
- Start thinking about what you want in a college.

Junior Year
- Take AP classes if you can.
- Do your best on the PSAT.
- Prepare for the SAT/ACT in the fall and take the exam in the spring.
- Take the SAT Subject Test for courses recently completed, such as Chemistry or U.S. History.
- Research colleges and financial aid opportunities.
- Begin visiting colleges that interest you.
- Identify what tests (i.e., SAT Subject Tests) the colleges that interest you require.
- Start asking for letters of recommendation.
- Over the summer, develop your interests even further. Consider a unique volunteer opportunity, or try to get a paying job.

Senior Year
- Take the SAT, ACT, and SAT Subject Tests for courses most recently completed.
- Request additional letters of recommendation from senior year teachers, if necessary.
- Send off college applications.
- Apply for financial aid.
- Wait for your acceptances to arrive in the spring.
- Start packing.

You're going to college, baby!

3 Grades
and the quality of your courses are more important than your SAT or ACT scores.

Get this—

The people who hold your college fate in their hands have a method to ranking applications. Here's the scoop:

Really, really, **really**, **really** important: G.P.A./
Class Rank/
Coursework

Really, really, **really** important: SAT/ACT Score

Really, **really** important: Essays

Really important: Teacher
Recommendations

Important: Extracurricular
Activities

Now that you know . . .

Use this info to your advantage!

- *Form good study habits early, and set the academic bar high.*
- *Prepare for the SAT/ACT and check out* **collegeboard.com** *or* **kaptest.com** *for test info.*
- *Join a club or volunteer your time to a cause that interests you.*
- *Develop your writing skills.*
- *Foster relationships with teachers early—remember, they'll be writing your recommendations.*

A note on class rank

Colleges view a high class rank as a strong indicator of academic potential. If your high school does rank its students, keep those grades up! If your high school doesn't rank students, don't worry— colleges won't hold it against you. Either way, maintaining a good G.P.A. is a sure way to win points with the admissions committee.

4 Go above and beyond the academic minimum.

Most **COMPETITIVE** colleges want students who not only do well, but also do well in **CHALLENGING** classes.

Think about . . .
. . . taking honors or advanced placement courses instead of regular classes

. . . taking four years of a single foreign language

. . . taking four years of math instead of three

. . . taking sciences that require lab work

Ready to work?

Only you can be the judge. Honors and AP classes are tougher than regular classes, but don't let your fear of a lower G.P.A. stop you. Many selective colleges give difficult coursework more weight than the easy stuff. You might surprise yourself! Plus, scoring high on AP exams can boost your academic profile and allow you to receive college credit for courses in those subjects.

AP Exams 101

The College Board offers AP exams in the following subject areas:

Chemistry

Art History

Biology

Calculus BC

Calculus AB

Computer Science AB

Computer Science A

Microeconomics

Macroeconomics

English Literature

English Language

European History

Environmental Science

French Literature

French Language

Comp Government & Politics

Human Geography

German Language

Latin: Vergil

U.S. Government & Politics

Latin Literature

Physics B

Psychology

Music Theory

Physics C

Spanish Literature

Spanish Language

Studio Art

Statistics

World History

U.S. History

Check out
collegeboard.com/student/testing/ap/about.html
for more info, test dates, and sample questions.

TIP 5

It's never too late to improve your grades.

Did freshman and sophomore years totally tank your grades? Don't give up. College admissions officers look at the whole picture—especially when it comes to your G.P.A.

Analyze this!

Reflect on where you went wrong. Ask yourself:

- Is the coursework really over my head?
- Am I doing all of my homework and studying for tests?
- Am I having trouble fitting homework, work, and extracurricular and social activities into my schedule?
- Are my friends doing well in the same classes? If not, why?
- Have I seen my teacher for extra help?

It's all in your head

Here's what you can do to get your grades going in the right direction:

1. <u>Ask for help:</u> Is your best friend a whiz in the subject? Maybe all you need is a pal to explain it. If that doesn't work, perhaps your parents can set you up with a tutor.

2. <u>Make a real commitment to do better in school:</u> That means no TV or IM-ing your buds until AFTER you've finished your masterpiece on the Revolutionary War.

3. <u>Consider dropping a demanding extracurricular activity:</u> It doesn't have to be forever, but maybe all you need is to spend some extra time hitting the books until the subject clicks.

4. <u>Hang out with successful students:</u> You never know—their study habits might rub off on you!

Become a better test taker.

Many students complain that they're just not good at taking the SAT or ACT, the very tests that help determine their academic future. But every student can improve his or her test-taking skills. Here's how:

1. Do NOT go into a test cold. Familiarize yourself with the exam. That means understanding the format and directions as well as knowing what kinds of questions will be asked.

2. Practice taking exams under test-like conditions. You can find free practice tests at **kaptest.com** to get you started.

3. Develop strategies for taking the SAT/ACT, such as knowing when to guess or how to backsolve a math equation.

4. Run through a practice test again . . . and again . . . and *again*—especially if you're someone who tends to freeze under pressure. The more you do it, the less nervous you'll be when you take the real thing.

5. Go into the test with confidence. A positive attitude goes a long way!

MYTH:

"If I get a low score on the SAT, I'll never get into college, and I'll be stuck flipping burgers for the rest of my life!"

MYTHBUSTER:

Relax. Your SAT/ACT score is not the only element of your application that determines whether or not you are accepted. Besides, there are thousands of great schools out there. One of them is bound to be the right fit for you.

7

Take the PSAT in your sophomore year—even though it doesn't count.

Huh? Take a test that doesn't count? Why would you **EVER** want to take a test that **DOESN'T** count?

Think about it

- *It doesn't matter if you totally blow it. When you take it again junior year, when it **DOES** matter, you'll know what to expect. Not to mention that you'll probably get a better score—and a better score means a better chance at getting a National Merit Scholarship®.*

- *Soon after the test, you will mysteriously begin to receive college catalogues and brochures about special programs, giving you a sneak peek at what's out there.*

- *They don't call it the SAT's kid brother for nothing. At the very least you'll get some extra practice for what can be an intimidating exam. And you know what practice makes…perfect!*

MYTH:

*"I took the PSAT in my sophomore year
and got a nearly perfect score. I'm so
glad I don't have to take it again!"*

MYTHBUSTER:

Sorry folks. You DO have to take it
again if you want to be eligible for some
scholarships. Remember, your
sophomore PSAT score doesn't count—
even if it is awesome.

A note on
National Merit Scholarships®

The National Merit Scholarship Corporation® hands out
over $50 million to more than 10,000 college (and college-
bound) students. You are automatically registered when
you take the PSAT, and will be notified if you are eligible
to participate in the program based on your PSAT score.
Then you must meet eligibility requirements (found on
nationalmerit.org).

8

Admissions officers use SAT and ACT scores to gauge your academic potential in college.

So, what can you do to rock the tests? Contrary to popular belief, you CAN study for standardized tests. Here's how:

1. Read!

2. Beef up your vocabulary and grammar skills.

3. Review algebra and geometry skills (and science too for the ACT).

4. Start a journal to improve your writing abilities.

5. Start an SAT study group with friends— it's easier to study with a buddy.

Be prepared

- Go to **collegeboard.com** to familiarize yourself with the structure of the SAT/ACT and download study materials.

- Go to the bookstore—there is a whole section of practice guides for standardized tests!

- Find out if your school offers SAT preparation.

- Ask a teacher or guidance counselor for help/suggestions.

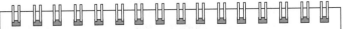

What the test-makers won't tell you . . .

Almost all competitive schools accept both SAT and ACT scores. What's the big deal? Well, the SAT is 2/3 critical reading and writing and 1/3 math. The ACT is 1/2 English and reading, and 1/2 math and science. So if you're strong in English, you might want to take the SAT. If you're awesome in math and science, but not so good in English, you might do better on the ACT.

Don't wait until junior year to take SAT Subject Tests.

SAT Subject Tests are designed to assess your achievment on high school subjects such as History, Math, Science, English, and Foreign Languages. You **KNOW** it's best to take **ANY** exam while the material is fresh in your mind—so why wait until you forget all of your geometry theorems to take the math Subject Test?

To test or not to test

Deciding which tests to take isn't that tough. Just make a list of the colleges you're interested in. Then check out their websites, catalogs, or viewbooks to find out how many Subject Tests they require and in which subjects.

Check it!

Not sure where you want to go to college? Take this checklist to your guidance counselor to help you figure out your SAT Subject Test future.

— Biology (Environmental/Molecular)

— Chemistry

— English Literature

— Foreign Language (Chinese, French, German, Italian, Japanese, Korean, Latin, Modern Hebrew, or Spanish)

— Math Level 1

— Math Level 2

— Physics

— U.S. History

— World History

Test-taker tip

You'll do better if you complete **AT LEAST** *two years of study before you take a foreign language Subject Test.* **¿Comprendes?**

10 Submit SAT Subject Test scores even if a college only recommends that you do so.

Hasn't your mom ever **RECOMMENDED** that you clean your room—and then grounded you for not doing it? Perhaps your teacher has **RECOMMENDED** that you look over your notes only to surprise you with a pop quiz the next day. Well, the same is true in the world of college applications and acceptances.

A few (ahem) recommendations . . .

1. Repeat this: "*Recommend* means 'I suggest you do it if you know what's good for you'!"

2. Review the list of colleges you want to apply to. Make sure that you have followed all of the colleges' recommendations.

3. While you're at it, check to see if your picks also give you the option to write a personal statement.

4. If so, we **RECOMMEND** that you write one of those, too.

SAT Subject Tests 101

SAT Subject Test scores are used by colleges to make admissions and/or placement decisions; for example, a high score on the Literature test may exempt you from an English requirement. Remember, each college requires certain scores for each recommended test, so find out what your score goal is before you start studying.

11 Team up to study for the SAT.

Studying with friends is a **PROVEN** score booster . . . and may even get you a date! Study groups keep you committed, help improve your skills, and stop you from worrying about the test.

Serious studying

1. Bring together a group of kids who are committed to preparing for the test.

2. Set realistic goals and stick to them.

3. Find a comfortable place to meet.

4. Now, get to work!

Serious strategies

- *Try quizzing each other with vocabulary flashcards.*

- *Take SAT quizzes and grade each other.*

- *Review a test prep book chapter and ask questions—if no one knows the answer, take it to a parent or teacher for clarification.*

Serious rewards

Nobody can spend every waking minute in study mode, right? So don't forget to schedule time for a little R&R (here's where the date part comes in). How about:

- a bowling expedition after completing your first practice test?

- going on a pizza run every time your group aces 50 tough vocabulary words?

- a movie marathon after you've written a few practice essays?

Reading is a natural SAT and ACT score booster.

It's true! Reading helps your score in two ways:

1. The more you read, the more you cultivate your comprehension skills.

2. Reading builds your vocabulary without you even trying!

Pick it up and read it!

Set a goal to read for at least 30 minutes every day. You'll be surprised at how easy it is to find the time!

Vocab in a flash

If you come across vocabulary you don't know, mark the word and look it up in the dictionary. Keep a list of all of the words you look up in, say, two weeks. Then you can make flashcards containing new words and their definitions for more vocab practice.

Reading doesn't have to be boring to be beneficial!

Check out your favorite:
- Comic books
- Teen book series
- Fashion mags
- Celebrity rags
- Newspapers
- Juicy beach reading
- Subway ads
- Cereal boxes
- Shampoo bottles

. . . get the idea?

Seek help from test-prep professionals when necessary.

For some, creating your own study schedule for yourself just doesn't cut it. Take the following quiz to see if you need a pro's help.

Do you:

Keep saying that you'll study for the SAT tomorrow?

___ yes ___ no

Have trouble understanding why you're getting questions wrong?

___ yes ___ no

Jump from topic to topic without focus?

___ yes ___ no

Find yourself unable to complete a section in the allotted time?

___ yes ___ no

If you answered "yes" to any of these questions, you might need a little structure to your SAT study time. A pro can streamline study time and teach you test-taking strategies.

Go pro!

- Check out a free review class offered by your school.

- Surf online for free test-taking tips.

- Purchase some professional SAT test-prep software for your computer.

- Attend a comprehensive SAT prep program.

- Peruse the test-prep section at your local bookstore.

- Research college admissions tutoring programs in your area.

The SAT is a big-time endurance test.

The SAT is **THREE HOURS and FORTY-FIVE MINUTES** *long.* *That's 225 minutes. Otherwise known as 13,500 seconds . . . You must learn how to build endurance and manage your time well in order to get a great score.*

Get the focus factor

1. <u>Start slowly.</u> Complete one section of a practice session. Time yourself and see how you do.

2. <u>Steady progression.</u> Develop your test-taking endurance by adding a section to your practice every day. For example, complete two sections, then three, and so on.

3. <u>Ready to marathon.</u> Now try an entire practice exam in one sitting. Set aside four hours and go for it!

4. <u>Keep it up!</u> Continue to build your endurance with practice tests until taking a nearly four-hour exam feels like no big deal.

SAT Exam Breakdown

Know the structure of the test to help you manage your time. You don't want to be caught with two minutes left in a section and only three questions answered!

Writing (Essay Writing): one 25-minute section

Writing (Sentence Error Identification, Sentence Improvement, and Paragraph Improvement): one 25-minute section

Writing (Sentence Improvement): one 10-minute section

Critical Reading (Sentence Completions and Reading Comprehension): two 25-minute sections and one 20-minute section

Math: two 25-minute sections and one 20-minute section

Experimental: one 25-minute section

Free your mind

Try this relaxing exercise to help focus on Test Day:

Take a deep cleansing breath and close your eyes. Starting with your eyebrows, gradually tighten every muscle in your body, ending with your toes. Hold it for a few seconds. Then relax one part at a time in reverse order. Open your eyes, and take another deep breath.

15

You can take the SAT or ACT more than once—in fact, you probably should!

Take the test for the first time in the spring of junior year. If you don't do as well as you'd like, then take it again in fall of senior year.

Chances are you will perform BETTER the second time around. Why?

- You already did it once, so you won't be as nervous.
- You identified your weaknesses and had time to strengthen them.
- You know the ins and outs of the test as well as the strategies you need to ace it.
- You will have completed more coursework and read more.

Who should and who shouldn't retake the exam?

Should:
- students who received low scores
- students who just missed making the numbers required by their colleges of choice
- students who froze during the test and know they can do better

Shouldn't:
- students who received a perfect or near-perfect score
- students who are confident that their numbers will hold up to the competition

A risk?

It's true that SOME schools combine your two scores if you retake the test, but 80% of schools evaluate only your top number. So, in the unlikely event you perform worse the second time around, it probably won't matter.

Colleges are looking for students who have passions.

Colleges don't necessarily want kids who belong to every club known to humankind.

In a word (or three), less is more. So grab a pen and paper and make a list of the things you love to do. Then go do them!

A club is what a club does

Some clubs sound great on paper but may not live up to your idea of cool. So if the Young Scientists Club meets once a month to talk about beakers when you'd rather be conducting research on the life cycle of the fruit fly, don't be afraid to talk to the club's president or advisor to suggest ways to improve the organization. But if your suggestions fall on deaf ears, it's OK to respectfully bow out and move on to bigger and better things.

Is it okay if . . . ?

. . . you're on the basketball, baseball, and wrestling teams? Yup. It shows you have a major passion for sports.

. . . you really, REALLY like solving quadratic equations in your spare time and belong only to the math club? Hey, you might be a Fields Medal-winning mathematician some day!

. . . you sample lots of different clubs your freshman and sophomore years, then continue on with only one or two? Uh-huh. You just had to figure out what you like, that's all!

MYTH:

"I've got to be super well-rounded if I want my top choice to even notice me!"

MYTHBUSTER:

Nope. Admissions officers are looking to create well-rounded campuses, so don't worry about joining the school newspaper if you'd rather spend all your time advocating for the rights of the duck-billed platypus. Go for it!

Don't join extracurricular activities just because they'll look good on a college application.

*If you aren't excited about what you're doing, chances are you won't perform well and will either a) quit or b) be miserable. Besides, once you have that interview with Joe Admissions Officer, he'll totally **KNOW** you weren't into that botany club you joined senior year.*

Are you in a club for the right reasons?

Before joining a club or activity, ask yourself:

 Am I really interested in what the club has to offer?

Will I have fun?

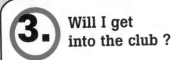

3. Will I get into the club?

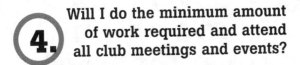

4. Will I do the minimum amount of work required and attend all club meetings and events?

5. Would I join it without my friends?

6.

Would I rather surf the Web, watch TV, or do homework than attend a meeting?

Your answers should be:

1. Yes

2. Yes

3. Yes

4. Yes

5. Yes

6. NO

18 Start your own club based on your own interests.

Why not? It's fun and you'll get major bonus points for doing your own thing— colleges like to see evidence of an entrepreneurial spirit.

Fresh ideas

- Organize a regular "Poetry Slam" at your local coffee house.

- Set up a pottery club.

- Work with a local community group to initiate a youth volunteer program.

- Start a record label.

- Create an environmental group.

Go clubbing!

- Check with the principal to make sure the club doesn't already exist. If it doesn't, find out what is required to set up a new club.

- Ask your favorite teacher to sponsor your group, and get permission from the principal if you want to have meetings on school grounds.

- Recruit club members by hanging flyers explaining your new club around school. (Don't forget to get permission first.)

- After you have a few members, schedule a meeting to plan your club's activities.

- Elect officers, and make plans to raise money if you need to.

- Have fun!

19 Make sure you're an active and involved student **BEFORE** senior year.

Aside from being able to respond with more than a blank stare when asked, "Where are all your extracurricular activities?" in a college interview, you'll find that you'll gain more from getting involved than you could ever imagine. So just do it—you **KNOW** *you want to!*

You be the judge:

Admissions officers can spot "last minute" activities a mile away. Can you?

Jane Smartypants
Captain, Debate Club, 4 years
Second chair flutist, Wind Ensemble, 3 years
Founder, Intramural Coed Volleyball Team, 2 years

OR

Jane Oopslforgottojoinclubs
Member, Key Club, 1 year
Founder, Snowboarding Club of Central Florida, 1 year

The **pros** of getting involved

1. Teachers will get to know you through your actions in and around school.

2. Trying new activities is the only way to figure out your likes and dislikes.

3. You will definitely make more friends if you do something such as help decorate for the Spring Fling—and you might even GO to the dance this time.

4. Maybe you'll discover a hidden talent. How will you ever know if you're a born shot-putter if you never try out for track and field?

5. You just might find your true calling in life! Guess how Howard Stern, the famous radio talk-show host, got his start? As a high school DJ!

The **cons** of getting involved

(Only) 1. You will most likely miss the *Oprah* show. But hey, that's what TiVo is for!

TIP

20

Volunteer your time to a worthwhile cause.

Volunteering will not only give you a "warm-and-fuzzy" feeling because you'll be helping others, it will also impress college admissions people, show you what it's like to work in the real world, and hey, might even lead to a scholarship or turn into a paying job someday. And, stick with it as long as you can—colleges want to see that you have dedicated a significant amount of time to a cause.

Quality AND quantity

On your activity resume (see tip #69), list the total hours you spent volunteering or number of projects completed. For example:

- Volunteer, Shadybrook Retirement Home
  Jan 2004-Sep 2005, 5 hours/week

- Volunteer, New York Cares
  6 urban renewal projects

The first step

Grab a pen and paper and make a list of your interests. For example: are you good with a hammer? Maybe you can build a house with Habitat for Humanity. Are sweet, furry creatures your thing? You might want to volunteer at a local animal shelter. Once you know what you want to do, then find out where to do it!

You can:

- Join a youth organization that focuses on community service such as your local YMCA, your place of worship, or Girl/Boy Scouts.
- Get involved in a volunteer group at school.
- Maybe your parents volunteer. If so—ask them if you can go along.
- Start your OWN volunteer program!
- Search the Internet to connect with one of the thousands of worthy causes.

No time?

You can still give back by volunteering for a specific event like a March of Dimes Walk-a-Thon or a 5K run for breast cancer.

Time management is crucial when planning for college . . . and attending college.

Too much on your plate?

There are 168 hours in a week, but sometimes it feels as if you don't have enough time to do it all. Maybe you really **DON'T.** Take this time management quiz to find out!

How many hours a week do you spend . . .

. . . sleeping? ____ hours

. . . eating? ____ hours

. . . showering/picking out your clothes/getting your hair to look just right? ____ hours

. . . getting from your home to school and from school to home? ____ hours

. . . actually in school? ____ hours

. . . doing homework and studying? ____ hours

. . . doing chores or running errands? ____ hours

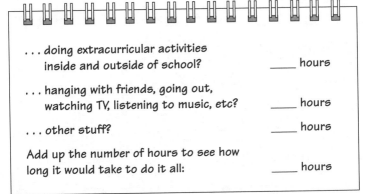

... doing extracurricular activities
inside and outside of school? _____ hours

... hanging with friends, going out,
watching TV, listening to music, etc? _____ hours

... other stuff? _____ hours

Add up the number of hours to see how
long it would take to do it all: _____ hours

Is your total:

LESS than 168 hours? You're managing time well.

MORE than 168 hours? You might not be using time wisely OR
you might have too much on your plate.

To get stuff off of your plate, keep track of each day's
activities and commitments—in other words, KEEP A
SCHEDULE. If your best friend calls to see if you want to go
with him to his sister's soccer game, check your schedule—if
you have already scheduled an SAT study session for that
time, say NO!

If you have trouble sticking to schedules (or love that snooze
button), enlist your friends and family to help you keep on
track and on time (i.e., ask a friend to call you one hour
after you get home from school to check that you are NOT
watching TRL). Learning to manage your time is a valuable
skill that will not only help you organize your college
application process, but will help ease your transition to
college life and prove useful for your adventures after
college.

Say hello to your new best friend … the daily planner!

High school is a busy time, between classes, friends, extracurricular activities, studying, family responsibilities, college prep, and the rest. It's tough keeping it all together without pulling your hair out.

A plan to plan

- If you don't already have a daily planner or electronic scheduler, get one.
- Mark down every test, assignment due date, appointment, deadline, interview, college visit, etc. so you know how to organize your life.
- Set up time to study, complete homework, and do a little college prep.
- Remember to schedule in some chill time with friends and family, too!

Sample After-School Schedule

2:15—3:00	*Extracurricular activity*
3:00—3:30	*Home from school*
3:30—4:00	*Snack/chill time*
4:00—5:30	*SAT prep*
5:30—6:00	*FREE*
6:00—7:00	*Dinner*
7:00—9:00	*Homework*
8:30—10:00	*Internet/Phone (maybe do some research on colleges or get started on your application essay)*
10:00—11:00	*TV/Reading (build that vocab!)*
11:00	*Bedtime!*

Take control

Just because you keep a schedule doesn't mean you have to give up all of your free time. You have weekends, remember? And keeping to a schedule will make your application process less overwhelming so you can spend less time stressing and more time getting closer to your goal—step by step.

Take time to explore different cultures . . . as well as your own.

Being culturally aware will not only teach you about yourself, it will open your eyes to the greatness of diversity.

Going global

1. Did your family originate in Italy or England or Puerto Rico or Japan? Follow your family tree back to your roots.

2. Learning French? Try a study abroad or work-exchange program in France.

3. How about joining an international volunteers program and doing community service in a country like Peru?

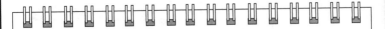

Parents won't let you go?
Funds tight?

Here are some ideas to go global from home:

1. Ask a parent or grandparent to tell you stories about your family's history, and create a family tree.

2. Attend a diversity program offered by your school or through a local college.

3. Rent foreign movies, and read books written by multicultural authors.

4. Download ethnic recipes, and have fun preparing special dinners with your friends.

5. Talk to exchange students studying at your school. Just listening to their stories will enrich your understanding of another culture.

Guess what?
Any and all of these experiences are great college essay topics.

24 Avoid senioritis*—even if you've already received an acceptance letter from your top college choice.

Why NOT take a little break? Many colleges make your admission offer conditional on maintaining your G.P.A. If it drops significantly, you might just get another letter telling you to stop packing.

*senioritis (seen yoor i tiss) *n.* 1. The quality or state of being totally uninterested in the academic portion of high school, usually suffered by graduating seniors. 2. The desire to goof off in class, spend hours playing Counterstrike, and/or create a masterful plot to kidnap the opposing football team's mascot at the expense of studying for finals.

Do

- Take challenging classes that will prepare you for college coursework.
- Stay involved in your school and community service activities.
- Consider an internship to start you on a possible career track.
- Start planning and packing for college.
- Read. You will be most likely be required to read some classic literature your freshman year—why not get a jump on it? For starters, you can try:

Crime and Punishment, Fyodor Dostoevsky, 1866

100 Years of Solitude, Gabriel Garcia Marquez, 1967

Catcher in the Rye, J.D. Salinger, 1951

Maus: A Survivor's Tale, Art Spiegelman, 1992

1984, George Orwell, 1949

Their Eyes Were Watching God, Zora Neale Hurston, 1937

Dubliners, James Joyce, 1914

Hiroshima, John Hersey, 1946

Pride and Prejudice, Jane Austen, 1813

Hamlet, William Shakespeare, c. 1601

Some of these books your professors will expect you to have covered in high school, some are guaranteed to be on the syllabi of introductory courses in your major, and some are simply stimulating reads that will help you to develop a more well-rounded knowledge of classic literature (and that won't hurt, no matter what your major).

Don't

- Designate every Friday as senior cut day.
- Slack off on homework and studying.
- Forget to enjoy the time you have left with your friends and teachers. You won't be a high school student much longer!

A little work experience never hurts!

A job in the real world can earn you some extra cash as well as show the college admissions folks that you can:

- keep a commitment
- manage time
- determine priorities

Who knows? You might also discover your future career or, at the very least, find out that you hate serving up lattes.

Do it!

Go to your local burger joint, mall, coffee house, etc., and ask if they need any help. If so, fill out an application. Consider applying for jobs that relate to your interests—maybe the physical therapy clinic needs a receptionist or the local newspaper is looking for an office assistant.

The perks

- *Ask about employee discounts—10% off CDs or books could really help your budget (and help you decide what to get people for their birthdays).*
- *Working gives you the opportunity to meet new people that you may not otherwise have a chance to encounter. And who knows, you could bump into your future prom date at work!*
- *If you perform well at work, you may be eligible for a raise!*

If you are interested in…	look for work at…
Law	*Legal firm, courthouse*
Computers	*Technology store, computer repair shop*
Writing	*Bookstore, library, newspaper*
Fashion	*Your favorite clothing store, fabric store*
Science/Engineering	*Pharmaceutical company, medical lab*
Biology/Ecology	*Zoo, aquarium, wildlife reserve, state park*
Art	*Museum, gallery*
Medicine/Health Services	*Hospital, doctor's office, public health outreach program*
Sports	*Athletic office of a local college, recreation center, camp*
Music	*Record store, recording studio, music magazine*

You get the idea!

Make the most of your summers.

Take part in fun and challenging activities that you can't fit in during the school year. Why? You'll definitely find tons to talk about at a college interview but, even better, you'll experience AMAZING summers and create lasting memories.

Your passion . . . with a twist!

Instead of putting your interest in acting aside for the summer, enter an acting-intensive summer camp to hone your talent.

- Why go back to the same old lifeguard job at your local beach when you might be able to get a work-exchange position in Australia?

- Get a taste of what it's REALLY like to go to college. Attend a course away from home, and stay in the dorms.

- Have a flair for foreign languages? Try spending a summer with a host family overseas.

Part Two:

Steps to Choosing the Right College for You

27 Look inside yourself.

Don't worry. You'll have lots of people telling you where **THEY** *think you should go to college. Before that begins, take a moment to figure out what* **YOU** *want.*

Visualize . . .

Go to your room and shut the door. Lie on the bed, close your eyes, and begin to dream of college.

What kind of campus do you see?

- A city landscape?
- A college surrounded by wilderness?
- Something in between?

What kind of classrooms do you see?

- large lecture halls?
- small, 12-person rooms?
- medium-sized rooms like you had in high school?

What kind of dorm life do you see?

- an ivy-covered brick dwelling on the perimeter of a grassy quad?
- a high-rise on a bustling city street?
- an off-campus apartment?

More questions

- What do I want to study? Do I want to go to a place that offers lots of options so I can try a few things before I decide on a major?
- Do I want to meet people that share my interests or people with different interests?
- Do I want to go to a single-sex or a coed college?
- Do I want to attend a small private college, a large university, or something in the middle?
- Do I want to take part in campus life? Am I interested in athletics or other extracurricular activities?
- Where do I want to live? Close to home? Far away? Somewhere in-between?

Apply to a minimum of six colleges.

The more colleges you apply to, the better chance you have at getting into one (or more) of them. And you'll never get into your dream college unless you **TRY** to get in!

The breakdown

You should apply to:

- **Two dream colleges**—*there's a chance that you can get in, but you're not 100% sure.*
- **Two realistic colleges**—*you meet the college's requirements and have an excellent chance of being accepted.*
- **Two safety colleges**—*you meet or exceed the college's requirements, so your chances are pretty good!*

Seek out colleges that best match your grades and test scores.

Check the chart below to see where you fall on the academic food chain.

	Most Competitive	Highly Competitive	Very Competitive	Competitive	Less Competitive	Not Competitive
Grade Average	A+/A	A-/B+	B+/B	B/B-	B-/C	C
Combined SAT Score*	1350-1600	1200-1350	1100-1200	900-1100	Below 900	--
SAT Subject Tests Required	Usually 3	Usually 3	1-3 tests strongly recommended	May be required	Not required	Not required
Typical Academic Requirements						
English	4 years	4 years	4 years	4 years	4 years	4 years
Math	4 years	3 years	3 years	3 years	2-3 years	2-3 years
History	4 years	4 years	4 years	4 years	4 years	4 years
Science	3-4 years	3-4 years	3 years	2-3 years	2-3 years	2-3 years
Foreign Language	4 years	3-4 years	3-4 years	3 years	2 years	--

*Score ranges reflect SAT socring scales for pre-March 2005 test administrations.

29

All colleges are not the same.

Learning about what's out there will help you narrow your search and build your confidence as you realize that there are colleges that are right for all types of students.

Two-year vs. Four-year Colleges:

Two-year colleges are commonly known as community colleges or junior colleges. These small and nurturing institutions often have open admission and are geared toward students who are looking to earn an associates or technical degree or to eventually transfer to a four-year college. Four-year colleges offer baccalaureate (and, often, graduate) degrees and often boast distinguished faculty, extensive course choices, and robust academic resources. Most allow students to commute but also offer on-campus housing as well as an array of extracurricular activities and campus organizations.

Public vs. Private Colleges:

Public colleges receive significant funding from the state in order to keep tuition low. Higher tuition is often charged to out-of-state residents. Private colleges are not publicly funded, so tuition is usually higher than public colleges. They rely on endowments to help keep costs down. You will recognize the names of some prestigious private colleges that are internationally known, like NYU, Stanford, or Northwestern.

Religiously Affiliated Colleges:

The association with a particular religion may be obvious in a school's name, or not. Students at these institutions are often required to attend religious classes of some kind, and faculty are often required to promote the church's beliefs.

Historically Black Colleges:

Typically, historically black colleges and universities offer a diverse student body and faculty, as well as an educational experience that nurtures a student's heritage, ethnicity, and interests.

Same-Sex Colleges:

These colleges offer a single-sex educational experience.

Specialty Colleges:

These colleges focus mostly on one area of study, such as art or business, offering the opportunity to completely immerse into a major. Music conservatories offer focused musical study in an elite environment, while technical colleges offer instruction in areas like computer technology and manufacturing.

Talk to your parents about your college expectations— and theirs—before you begin your search.

Get on the same page

1. Sit your parents down for "the talk." The financial one, that is. You want to know if your parents can afford tuition and, if so, how much. This information will affect your college search parameters. Don't, however, give up on a college based on its price tag—find out specifics about their financial aid first!

2. Discuss your preferences to either commute from home or to live in a dorm on campus. Then ask your parents what they think. Remember, there are housing and meal plan fees that you and your parents will have to consider if you want to live on campus.

3. Find out if your parents have any restrictions on how far away you can go for college. Mention local colleges in which you might be interested.

4. Discuss any disagreements, and try to come to an agreement on your college options—communication is key to compromise.

Remember

Months into your search, you don't want to find out that your parents have opinions that dramatically differ from yours.

Don't forget to use your school's resources. Hey, they're free!

*Would you believe it? High school guidance counselors say that some students have **NEVER** stepped into their office to even look through a catalog!*

4 things to do in your friendly neighborhood guidance counselor's office:

1

Make an appointment to actually TALK one-on-one with your counselor. You can discuss what you're looking for in a college, how your grades and test scores fit into the mix, learn about financial aid, scholarships, and more. You'll find it's a lot easier to do this whole college thing when you have somebody on your side that understands the process.

Check out a college guide.

2. It's like a "phone book of colleges" that provides a whole bunch of statistics and maybe even a student opinion or two about the colleges of your choice. Flip through randomly at first. Before you know it you'll be coming back again and again to look up info on colleges that stand out.

3. **Go online.** Check out college websites for information on specific academic programs, student life, famous alums, and much, much more. Check out some search programs such as *collegeboard.org*, *fastweb.org*, and many others.

Take an Interest Assessment Quiz. **4.**
For one thing, it's fun. For another, it could point you in the direction of your dream college.

TIP

32

Keep the "Six Factors to Finding a College" in mind.

Factor in . . .

1. **Academics:** Consider the college's educational value, availability of majors, number and quality of faculty, and its overall reputation.

2. **Location:** Do you want to study in a rural location, where there are fewer distractions but fewer off-campus activities? Or are you into suburban or city life, where there are more internship opportunities but at the cost of expensive housing and higher crime rates? Climate can also be a factor if you're going to stray far from home—if you're thinking about Northwestern, you'd better be prepared for those sub-arctic Illinois winters!

3. **Size:** Pretty self-explanatory—small, medium, or super-sized.

4. **Campus life:** Make sure the college supports your lifestyle—academically **and** socially. After all, you won't be studying 24/7. If you want to play football, make sure your prospective college has a football team!

5. **Special services:** If you are a student with learning or other disabilities, be sure the campus offers the appropriate support.

6. **Cost:** Consider tuition and room & board, of course. Also, a college may require you to pay fees for equipment and labs, health services, parking, and nonresident fees (if you live out-of-state). Don't forget to budget for textbooks and travel expenses (if you go to college far from home).

Do it!

Find out if your favorite colleges measure up to your Six Factors standard.

33

Develop a well-rounded wish list of colleges based on solid research—not hype.

5 tips to start "the list"

1. Ask family members where they went to college and how they liked the experience.

2. Talk to recent high school graduates to find out how college life is going for them.

3. Attend at least one local "College Night," and pick up as many publications as you can carry.

4. Spend an afternoon going through college brochures and websites.

 5. Jot down the names of colleges that seem to have what you're looking for.

5 tips to make "the list" solid

1. Check out prospective colleges in a college directory to see if they match your academic criteria and that you are close to matching theirs.

Take virtual campus tours via official college websites. **2.**

3. Visit general college websites for secondary information on desirable schools.

Take the time to read course descriptions, areas of academic research, faculty bios, and career placement opportunities in your prospective major. **4.**

5. Visit campuses in person.
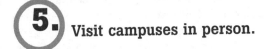

TIP
34

Go virtual with your college search.

*Begin your college search on the right foot. Download valuable information from one of the big college search engines such as **collegeboard.com** or **fastweb.com** where you'll find thousands of statistics along with college prep, career, and financial aid info.*

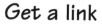

Get a link

Once you've sifted through the stats, link to official college websites to learn about majors and requirements, view pictures of the campus, and find out about the faculty, student services, and whatever else you're interested in. To get a well-rounded view of a college, be sure to check out:

- the student newspaper, to see what issues concern the student body and what's going on around campus
- the athletic department home page, to learn about the college's varsity teams and schedules, as well as their intramural programs and fitness facilities
- the calendar of events at the campus arts center, to find out what kinds of musical and theatrical events take place on campus
- recent press releases from the campus information department, to read about new buildings and programs, student and faculty awards and honors, and achievements in sports, among other newsworthy items

Personal virtual

Now it's time to get the "unofficial" take on your top picks. Log on to the websites below to get a personal perspective on your favorite colleges:

campusdirt.com: A fun site that not only offers you the usual college comparisons and financial aid search engines, but also connects you with behind-the-scenes info about what life on the various campuses is REALLY like.

collegeconfidential.com: A great college search engine with cool top ten lists and more. One highlight is the message board where you can talk to other students (and parents too) about the stress of getting into a college, among other things. They also offer college counseling (for a fee) if you need additional help choosing a college.

studentsreview.com: Here you'll get—you guessed it—student reviews of colleges as well as links to related sites.

teenink.com: Read college reviews and essays—written BY students FOR students—as well as opinions on a whole lot of other stuff. Don't forget to check out the cool bulletin board where you can rant and rave about your college search or just jot down your deepest thoughts for all to see.

Remember

Don't spend **ALL** your time surfing the Internet for college information. Talk with your counselor, too!

35

Don't rely on college rankings alone.

Several educational and media organizations rank colleges in terms of several criteria, including matriculation and graduation rates, curriculum breadth and depth, cost of tuition and fees versus financial aid packages, special programs and services, extracurricular activities, and minority enrollment (among many others). A college's rank may play a part in your decision to apply, but keep the following in mind before you check out the top ten colleges:

1. No college has an excellent program in every major or serves every conceivable need.

2. Curriculum, amenities, and faculty change over time.

3. Rankings alter from year to year and are, to a certain extent, subjective.

Create your OWN top ten list!

Make sure your list includes colleges that:

- cater to your interests
- challenge you academically
- will nurture your specific career goals
- have environments that feel comfortable

MYTH:

"I got accepted to all of my colleges—including Harvard. I didn't get that "warm-and-fuzzy" feeling when I visited the campus, but I guess my decision is made. I mean, it's HARVARD!

MYTHBUSTER:

Just because you can get INTO a college, doesn't mean it's the RIGHT CHOICE for you.

36

Ask yourself the most important question: Will I really fit in at this campus?

Fitting into a college's social environment is critical to a student's happiness.

If the shoe doesn't fit

If the thought of joining a fraternity makes your skin crawl, check the percentage of undergraduates that go Greek at your top choices. If it's more than 30%, you may want to reconsider! Ask yourself the following questions. Your answers will help you determine what type of social environment you'll be most comfortable in:

- Do I take academics seriously and want fellow students to do the same?
- Are athletics important to me and can I play my sport at the college I like?
- Do I want to join a fraternity or sorority?
- Do I want to stay on a contained campus that is similar to my high school?
- Do I want to mix socially with people from other colleges?
- Do I want to spend a lot of time partying?
- Do I want to meet people unlike myself?

Fitting in

Draw a line to match the student type to the college that seems most appropriate for each type.

1. A serious opera singer who has her sights set on Carnegie Hall.

2. A brilliant social activist looking for a few good issues to defend.

3. A conservative southern girl who can't wait to explore sorority life.

4. A born leader, looking for a career in the army and free tuition.

5. A smart and serious girl with an interest in women's studies.

6. A student that wants to be free to make up his own major and gets annoyed when people stare at his piercings.

UC Berkeley

West Point

Juilliard School

Washington and Lee University

New York University

Wellesley College

Answers

1. Juilliard School, 2. UC Berkeley, 3. Washington and Lee University, 4. West Point, 5. Wellesley College, 6. New York University

How'd you do? If some of the answers confuse you, look up the colleges listed here for more information, and see if the matches start making sense.

37

Go where the admissions reps are—go to a college fair!

Ask your guidance counselor when the next local fair is coming up. Also, check out the National Association for College Admission Counseling website (**nacac.com**) to find out when the next national fair in your area will be held. These events can be a bit overwhelming—especially the biggies run by the NACAC—but with a little planning, you'll get all the info you need.

Personal plan of attack

Before

1. Look over the list of participants.
2. Mark the colleges that you'd like to learn about.
3. Write down a few questions for the college representatives.
4. Print up some self-adhesive labels with your name, address, phone number, email address, high school, graduation year, intended major (it's OK to put undecided), and any extracurricular activities you're interested in pursuing. These labels are particularly handy because instead of filling out a ton of college information cards by hand, you can just stick

your labels on the cards and spend more time learning about colleges.

5. Stick your lists, labels, a pen, and a pad into a backpack (a large one for all of the info you'll be bringing home) to take to the fair.

During

1. Look for a map of where each college is located, and plan out a direct route so you'll have time to visit all the colleges on your list—grab all the brochures and catalogs you can carry.

2. Write down a few thoughts about each college and the answers to your questions as soon as you leave a booth. Then move on to the next table on your route.

3. Browse the colleges that didn't make it onto your list. Don't just stick to the booths that seem popular. You never know—a college you've never heard of might just be everything you're looking for.

4. Start at the far end of the room; everyone begins talking to colleges near the entrance of the fair, so beat the crowds by working the room in reverse!

5. Talk to admissions representatives. Indicate your interest in the college, and ask intelligent questions. When you are finished, ask the rep for a business card—he/she could be a valuable contact in the future.

6. If available, check out an info session on financial aid or applying to colleges.

After

1. Re-read your notes and start plowing through all those brochures you collected.

2. Make a list of the colleges that you're STILL interested in.

3. Start scheduling some visits (If you or your parents are members of AAA, they can help you design your college tours).

4. Email or write admissions officers that you met at the fair to thank them for sharing information with you and express your continued interest in their college.

38 Don't fall for marketing ploys.

Weeks after completing your college entrance exam, you'll start to receive colorful brochures and inspiring letters from admissions officers who TRULY believe THEIR college is "the one." Don't fall for it.

All that stuff is flattering at first . . . until it begins to pile up in the family room. The reality? Higher education is a business, and colleges are simply marketing to their target audience—you.

Be realistic

The brochure arrived with all the others. After one look at the front cover, you're convinced that the U of Surfing, situated on a cliff overlooking the Pacific Ocean, is the one for you. You can picture it now: studying biology in your board shorts, reading Shakespeare at the surf shack, talking social theory with your classmates as you stroll along a sandy path in the sunlight—SNAP OUT OF IT! Why? For one, U of S offers three majors, and strawberry farming strays a bit from the journalism major you've been preparing for. Two, your mother will have a fit if her baby moves 3,000 miles away from her. And three, your SAT scores are well OVER the accepted range at U of S—will you really be challenged academically?

Little by little

1. Go through your college mail every day so that it doesn't pile up (and so your parents won't nag you about it).

2. Separate the brochures that "speak to you" and place them in a "to research" file. (Don't forget to do the research!)

Look out for hidden gems. Go beyond the smiling faces on the front of the brochure and read about academics and internships. You might find a couple of cool colleges you never knew existed. **3.**

4. Toss the rest (into the recycling bin, please!), or share them with your guidance office—there may be another student who is interested in the applications, catalogs, or viewbooks that don't interest you.

Don't let impossibly high tuition stop you from applying to a pricey college.

Why bother doing the research if you KNOW you can't pay for it? Well, for one thing, who says YOU'RE going pay for it all?

Think about it

1. Colleges that want you to attend will most likely offer you some sort of financial aid if you need it.

2. There are tons of private scholarship programs that donate funds based on criteria ranging from heritage to employment to what kind of toppings you like on your pizza.

3. Uncle Sam wants you to go to college too. Need-based federal and state grants are there for the taking.

4. There's always the infamous student loan (okay, so this one you have to pay back).

5. Many colleges offer work study programs in which you receive minimum wage in exchange for doing useful work on campus.

Check it

Still doubtful? Kaplan's *Guide to the 331 Most Interesting Colleges* puts you in the know when it comes to how generous colleges are with financial aid packages. You'll also find out the average loan debt a student will incur by the time he or she graduates from a college.

Go get it

____ *Explore scholarship and grant opportunities on the Internet. There are hundreds of websites (**finaid.org** is a good one) that offer info on college scholarships as well as searches to help you find the ones for which you qualify.*

____ *Browse through the tons of books at the library or in your guidance counselor's office devoted to the mysteries of financial aid.*

____ *Fill out a FAFSA (Free Application for Federal Student Aid), even if you don't think you'll qualify for assistance. Some colleges even require that parents fill out these forms to receive merit (free) money, so it's a good idea that they take an hour or two and make sure it is filled out. (See tips #81–86 for more info on the FAFSA and other financial aid options.)*

Prepare for parental pressure—and learn how to duck when it comes flying right at you.

Parents mean well—they really do. But sometimes they can be a real drag when it comes to "helping you" choose a college, especially if they're trying to convince you to go to their alma mater.

Here's how to get around it

1. Do the research on your favorites and theirs. Make sure you don't want to attend their alma maters because they're not right for you—not just because you want to be different from Mom or Dad.

2. Speak intelligently about the colleges that DO interest you. Show your parents that you're taking college seriously and that you have tangible reasons for liking your top picks.

3. Be assertive, not overly emotional. If you don't want to attend your parents' old colleges, tell them (nicely). But it's not okay to blow up at them—even if they're really pressuring you—because a) they're your parents, b) it will make you seem immature and turn your clever argument into mush, and c) they'll probably be paying the college bills.

Get your ducks in a row

Check out these scenarios for ideas:

<u>The pressure:</u> Dad keeps talking about how great his alma mater was when he went, and did he tell you that Grandpa went there too? Want to see his varsity basketball jacket?

<u>The duck:</u> Say that it sounds like it was cool, but your top choice has a cutting edge research facility, which is great because you want to major in molecular biology. Also, they've got a top-ranked crew team, and you really want to continue rowing after high school.

<u>The pressure:</u> During a tour of your number one pick's off-campus housing, Mom spots a pile of empty beer bottles outside a fraternity house. Mom is not amused. She thinks the university is too big and nothing but a party college. She reflects on how nice it was to go to a small women's college where she got lots of personal attention.

<u>The duck:</u> Take a deep breath. Tell Mom that her alma mater sounds great, but you want to attend a large college because you're not sure what your major should be. Her college just doesn't offer the variety of courses you need to figure it out. Also, tell Mom that since she raised you so well, she won't have to worry about you joining the drunken masses.

<u>The pressure:</u> You're super psyched that you got in to your top choice, which happens to be 634 miles from home. It's clear that Mom wants you to stay local and commute to a junior college nearby. She's gone so far as to leave a course catalog in your backpack with a note that says, "Please don't leave me!"

<u>The duck:</u> Have a heart-to-heart with Mom. Explain why you want to attend your top choice: not only is it the "best fit" for you academically, but you also think it's important to gain a "total experience" from college, which includes learning what it's like to balance your time and money and to make decisions on your own. Besides, you're going to miss her too and call every week . . . right?

<u>The pressure:</u> Dad is literally sweating over the price tags of the private colleges you're interested in. He insists that you apply to only state schools because there's no way he can afford the tuition, let alone room, board, and books.

<u>The duck:</u> Hand Dad a towel and explain the beauty of financial aid packages. Start off by showing him tip #39 in this book. Then wow him with the scholarship research you've already begun to apply for online. He'll be proud to see you're taking tuition into account too.

41

Stop obsessing over that one "perfect" college.

If you convince yourself that you will only be happy at one college, you're more likely to be extremely disappointed if you don't get in. Plus, you never really know how you will feel about a college until you go....

Get a grip

Having a dream college is great, BUT

- Make sure your list has more than one college on it.
- Add three or four colleges that seem to be a good match for you, then explore their websites and brochures to get a well-rounded view of them—you never know what you'll find that might make one of them a "dream" too!
- While you're at it, pick one or two "safety colleges" to round out the list—you want to head to school in September, right? If you apply to colleges that you are 99% sure to get into, you'll pretty much guarantee that you will be going.

Eggs...basket...

You know the saying "don't put all of your eggs in one basket"? Well, it's true. A student with her heart SET on Dartmouth was devastated when she was not admitted early decision. Since she had spent all of her effort on her Dartmouth application, she had to scramble to come up with other colleges she might want to attend, and ended up missing some of their application deadlines. (Happy ending: She did get into Tufts, and ended up spending four great years there. Go Jumbos!)

What do students REALLY think?

Each year, the National Survey of Student Engagement (NSSE) obtains information from hundreds of American colleges and universities about student participation in college-sponsored programs and activities to shed light on how undergraduates spend their time and what they gain from attending college. Find out if your college picks participate in the NSSE, and ask for the results. You'll find out what students **really** think of their colleges. This may help you add colleges to your list.

You can still achieve great success in life even if you don't have an Ivy League degree.

No room left at Harvard or Yale? Don't despair. According to a recent study, if you possess these three character traits, you'll be a success no matter what college you go to:

☐ *Persistence*

☐ *Charm*

☐ *Humor*

Check 'em off! You know you have 'em!

Just the facts

- Most American presidents did not attend Ivy League colleges.
- Harvard and Yale are not the alma maters of the majority of rich and powerful Americans.
- Influential alumni, who might help you in the real world, have graduated from just about every university in the United States.
- There are hundreds of lesser-known colleges with outstanding academic reputations. Just think of all the excellent students and professors that got rejected by the Ivy League. They had to go to college somewhere!

Famous and influential people… and their non-Ivy alma maters

Martin Luther King, Jr.	*Boston University*
Philip Glass, composer	*University of Chicago*
Larry Page, co-founder of Google	*University of Michigan*
Julie Taymor, film director	*Oberlin College*
Marion Jones, Olympic Gold Medalist	*University of North Carolina*

43 Call ahead to schedule a guided campus tour.

You've done the research on your favorite colleges. Now, you need to see firsthand what each college is like. However, going it alone might make these campuses seem like just a bunch of boring buildings. Take a campus tour—a student guide will not only show you around, he'll also show you the personality of the campus so you can picture yourself living and learning there.

Don't be shy—ask your guide the scoop on:

- the best place to study (it might not be the library)
- the nicest dorms
- the coolest on-campus jobs
- the tastiest cafeteria food
- where students hang out on campus
- athletic games and events
- upcoming concerts
- celebrity speakers
- whatever!

After the tour

Stick around for a few minutes to talk to the tour guide. If you're lucky, you might get some insight on more personal things such as:

- making new friends
- transitioning from high school classes to college coursework
- how to learn in a not-so-intimate lecture hall
- awesome and not-so-awesome professors
- joining a fraternity or sorority

Use your time wisely

You can turn an average tour into an amazing one just by asking a few questions. Hey, you might even inspire other prospective students to inquire about things they never thought to ask.

Attention Mom and Dad!

The campus visit is a highly personal experience. Let your child take the lead and ask the majority of questions. Limit yourself to no more than three questions; for example, it is perfectly appropriate to ask about financial aid, campus safety, and academic opportunities. Try to walk at least six steps behind the groups of students on the tour—let your child have the front seat!

Make sure to schedule a college visit when classes are in session.

This way, you get to see the good, the bad, and the ugly while the place is in full swing.

Pick a date . . . any date

- Ideally, a visit should occur in May of your junior year or in late August/early September of your senior year. Many colleges have begun classes during that time, while most high schools have not.

- Avoid visiting a college during exam weeks, or on weekends. Otherwise, you won't get an accurate picture of the place. If this is not possible, schedule a second visit when classes are in session.

Stuff these things into your backpack the day of the tour—you just might need them!

____ notebook and pen

____ digital camera

____ campus map and catalog

____ bottle of water and a snack

____ a list of places you don't want to miss

____ umbrella (if it's overcast)

____ a bunch of questions

3 in 1

See if you can schedule an informational interview with an admissions officer the same day you're touring the campus. And, if they offer appointments, visit the Financial Aid office, too.

What to wear

Plan to dress in "business casual" clothing on your college visits. Guys should wear the equivalent of khakis and a golf shirt, and girls should wear nice trousers or a skirt with a conservative top—no bare midriffs, please! Avoid wearing clothing that advertises other colleges. Remember to wear comfortable shoes since you will be walking most of the day!

45 Look for colleges that offer courses and activities in more than one area of interest.

Let's face it. Students change their minds—and their majors—all the time.

You've got it covered, right?

- You hate cold weather but you want to attend University X because your favorite writer is a professor there.
- You should go to College Y because it's got an awesome premed program. Okay, so the place is small; they don't offer the journalism or computer science classes you're interested in, but the premed stuff makes up for all of it.
- Big city life isn't your cup of tea, but Z University is the only place for a serious actor such as yourself. You don't mind sacrificing your track and field career or your mom's chocolate chip cookies for art. Really.

But what happens if

. . . your favorite writer decides to take time off from teaching to write his or her next masterpiece? You'll be stuck wearing an itchy wool sweater when you'd rather be reading 18th Century English Literature—on the beach.

. . . you find your gross anatomy lab, well, gross, and you realize that medicine is not for you? You might have to spend a semester staring at yucky stuff in formaldehyde when you could have been learning computer programming.

. . . that big city campus culture (or lack thereof) makes you miss your family more than you thought? You'll have to imagine your mom's cookies baking in the dorm's kitchen until you fly home for winter break.

TIP 46

Learn how you deal with stress—it may affect your decision.

Like it or not, the stress of getting into a college is nothing compared to the stress you'll experience once you actually get there. Even the best students are often shocked by the amount of work it takes to keep up in class. Try to find out the typical workload of the students at your prospective colleges, and be realistic about what it might do to your nerves. After all, you **DO** *want to get a quality education, but you* **DON'T** *want to be overwhelmed for four years.*

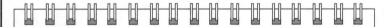

Test your stress

1. The thought of writing a 25-page paper on 18th Century English Literature makes you want to

   a) Hurl, and then you do.

   b) Hurl, but you head to the library instead. You've got a lot of research to do.

   c) Jump for joy. You love writing!

2. You think reading 75 pages per night for one class is

   a) Totally insane. How do people DO it?

   b) Tough, but you'll get it done, even if you have to stay up all night.

   c) So cool! You love reading!

3. You know you have to take three exams in one week. As you study you

a) Sweat, worry about failing, pig out, worry about failing, bite your nails, worry about academic probation. . . .

b) Are so glad you joined an awesome study group—it makes the work more manageable.

c) Do your infamous happy dance. You love taking tests!

If you answered mostly

a) You're a complete stress bunny. You might want to reconsider going to a college whose students are super competitive in academics.

b) You have a good head on your shoulders. We all know college is a challenge, but, hey, you're up for it.

c) You have no concept of stress . . . or reality. You would do very well at a fictional college.

The bottom line

- *Make sure the college you choose is a challenge.*
- *Make sure you can handle it.*
- *Make sure you can be happy.*

Community colleges are not just for "safety!"

Three reasons to love local learning

1. You can test the waters. The great thing about community college is that it's flexible. Whether you're still in high school or you're not so sure about your academic skills, you can find out if you're college material by taking just one class. If you need a little extra help, you'll be in the right place. Many community colleges offer small class sizes, where you'll find all the personal attention you need.

2. It's a stepping stone. You can attend a community college for a year or two, then transfer to a four-year university to gain a bachelor's degree. Or maybe you want to go for a two-year associate's degree or graduate from a certificate program that will train you for the workforce. A community college just might be the ticket!

3. Can you say, "debtless education?" If the idea of four years of mounting debt makes you queasy, you can definitely turn to a community college for a quality education. Why? For one thing it's typically inexpensive, yet it offers many of the same classes as the larger institutions. Also, you'll probably find a community college that's close to home, so you won't have a room and board expense. If you still have your heart set on going to a larger college but don't want to break the bank, consider taking your general requirements on the local level, then transferring the credits to the university of your choice. (Note: Be sure to find out first if your intended college will accept the credits.)

Community College Checklist

☐ Take a tour of the community college campus.

☐ Ask if you can sit in on a class to see how it feels.

☐ Check out scholarship and financial aid opportunities (yup, community colleges offer this stuff, too).

48

Don't make friends the deciding factor.

*It's one thing if you and your best friend have similar academic and social interests and wind up attending the same college. It's a whole other problem, though, if you choose to **FOLLOW** him or her because you don't want to feel lonely.*

What to do?

1. Be real. If you can't answer the question "Why do I want to go to this college?" then you're probably interested for the wrong reasons.

Try a mini separation. Go visit a college on your own for the weekend and see what it feels like. Is it really so awful to be without your friend? **2.**

3. Remember that you live in the "Information Age." Picture cell phones, email, text messaging . . . even if you're on opposite ends of the world, you'll still be connected!

Absence makes the heart grow fonder

Think about all the fun you'll have with your best friend when you're both back from college over Thanksgiving break. You can share pictures of your dorm-mates and regale each other with crazy college stories. Just because you are no longer joined at the hip doesn't mean you can't maintain that best friendship. Plus, it'll give you an excuse to get away from campus for the weekend and check out your friend's college experience.

Reverse reaction

Don't reject a college that you want to attend because your best friend is going there. Just because you're on the same campus doesn't mean you can't both spread your wings.

If you like a college, visit the campus a second time...or as many times as you like!

This time skip the guided tour and get down with the students!

A great time to interview

Something to consider when scheduling a second visit: Smaller colleges often offer students the opportunity to sit down face-to-face with an admissions officer—in other words, they offer a college interview. Although a successful interview will not guarantee admission, it will put a face with your name, which will help you as admissions officers discuss your application. To schedule an appointment, call the admissions office AT LEAST three weeks in advance (make sure to get directions to the office!).

Second visit checklist

Don't walk around campus aimlessly.
Use this checklist as a guide to get
you in gear.

___ Sit in on a class of a subject that
interests you.

___ Talk to a professor after class.

___ Grab a coffee at the student union, and
check out the college newspaper.

___ Talk to some students. Ask them what they
like and don't like about the college. Ask
them what they do for fun on the weekends.

___ Sit in an outdoor quad and people watch.

___ Browse in the college bookstore.

___ Walk or drive around the community
surrounding the campus.

___ Check out a dorm you didn't get to see
your first time around.

___ Spend the night in a dorm if the college
allows.

___ Imagine yourself as a student.

___ Talk to people that are involved with your
extracurricular activities—coaches, club
advisors, theatre directors, and
orchestra/band leaders are great contacts!

Put all your college facts in one place.

Use the following chart to create college "snapshots"—then you can easily compare and contrast important features and information. This will help you decide which college to choose.

College Name _____ _____ _____

General

Location? _____ _____ _____

Public/Private? _____ _____ _____

Religious
Affiliation? _____ _____ _____

# of Undergrads? _____ _____ _____

Freshman
Retention Rate? _____ _____ _____

Academics

Tough/
Manageable/Easy _____ _____ _____

Workload? _____ _____ _____

Class Size? _____ _____ _____

Majors of
Interest? _____ _____ _____

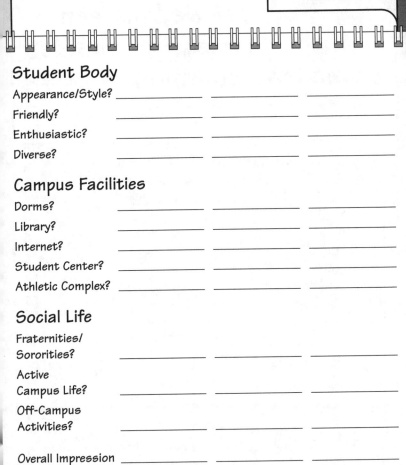

Student Body

Appearance/Style? _____ _____ _____

Friendly? _____ _____ _____

Enthusiastic? _____ _____ _____

Diverse? _____ _____ _____

Campus Facilities

Dorms? _____ _____ _____

Library? _____ _____ _____

Internet? _____ _____ _____

Student Center? _____ _____ _____

Athletic Complex? _____ _____ _____

Social Life

Fraternities/
Sororities? _____ _____ _____

Active
Campus Life? _____ _____ _____

Off-Campus
Activities? _____ _____ _____

Overall Impression _____ _____ _____

TIP

51

When trying to decide between colleges, consider some less common comparison factors.

Equal playing field?

If all the major factors between your top choices are on par, consider these possible features—some serious, some silly:

1. What kind of financial aid package are they offering?

2. Are there interesting internships available through the college?

3. What kind of career placement does the college offer?

4. Is there a study-abroad program?

5. Did the other students seem happy?

6. Does the campus have adequate security?

7. Which college had the best resident halls?

8. Are the guys/girls hot?

9. Can I find a good cup of coffee on campus?

10. Can I get a late-night pizza if I want to?

11. Do I like the college colors?

A dorm is a dorm is a dorm...or is it?

Where you live freshman year will affect your experience at college. Make sure you are comfortable with your options, and be prepared to adjust your expectations if you don't get housing in "the" freshman dorm. Would you be comfortable living in a single-sex dorm? Near the sports complex? In a non-freshman dorm? In a hotel? (Yes, it's possible, especially on urban campuses!) Sometimes, housing offices need to shuffle freshmen around in order to house all matriculated students. Consider housing factors as you try to decide between colleges.

If all else fails . . .

*...and you just cannot decide, ask your parents what **they** think!*

52

When logic fails, trust your instincts.

Be intuitive

1. Close your eyes and ask yourself the following question: Where do I feel I should go?

2. Follow your gut.

So, you think your instincts might be off? Try this!

1. Write the name of each college on a piece of paper and fold it in two.

Throw the papers into a hat or box or whatever.

3. Pick out one and look at it.

4. If you're disappointed, go to the other college.

If not, you just chose your college! **5.**

MYTH:

"This is the biggest decision of my life. If I choose the wrong college, I'll be totally miserable!"

MYTHBUSTER:

It's definitely a big decision, but if your colleges are pretty much equal, chances are that you'll be perfectly happy on either campus. You can create a positive college experience almost anywhere by what you put into it—get involved, pay attention, attend events, meet new people!

If by chance you *do* make a mistake in your choice of school, transferring is not the end of the world.

Really. It's no biggie. Lots of students do it.

Turn a negative into a positive

- You had to see first hand what you **DON'T** want to figure out what you **DO** want.
- If you have done well academically at the WRONG college, you might get into an even better RIGHT college.
- You are probably a stronger person than you were before.
- The application process will be easier.

Work it out

1. *Evaluate what it is that you don't like about your college.*
2. *Ask yourself how switching colleges will help.*
3. *Clearly identify your goals. What do you want to happen at your new college?*
4. *Find a college that will suit your newly defined needs.*
5. *Go for it!*

Part Three:

Helpful Relationships

Don't forget—
Parents have
feelings, too.

Mood swings

High hopes for you versus fear for
your safety. . . pride over the big
step you're about to take and
sadness about your taking that step
and leaving the nest . . . the desire
to help you get into the best college
possible but not wanting to overstep
the boundaries. These are just a few
of the conflicting thoughts that your
parents might be having. Applying
to college can be an emotional
roller coaster for you AND your
parents.

How do they cope?

Some pay attention to every minute detail of your college search and application process, trying to control everything.

Some may not want to get involved at all—except to ask, "Which college am I dropping you off at next August?"

Most parents fall somewhere in between the two extremes. Even so, your relationship with them is bound to run into a few bumps during this time.

How do YOU cope?

Have a heart-to-heart with your parents about your feelings. Don't be afraid to tell them if you need a bit more (or less) support. Then be specific with some things that they might do to make a change. Try to appreciate their perspective. After all, facing the "empty nest" is a big change for them, too!

"Own" your college application process.

Let your parents in on college decisions; don't let them make decisions for you.

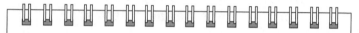

Work it, own it, work it, own it...

"Owning" the whole getting into college thing doesn't mean that you have to know what you're doing 24/7 or even figure everything out all by yourself. It DOES mean that you have to take responsibility for the process.

Do you "own" your college application process?

1. Do you look at your college list and wonder where some schools are located?

___ Yes ___ No

2. Do you have a dusty pile of unopened college mail somewhere in your house?

___ Yes ___ No

3. Did your mom/dad/counselor nag you to write your personal statement?

___ Yes ___ No

4. Do you forget your guidance counselor's name?

___ Yes ___ No

5. Did someone else set up your college interview?

___ Yes ___ No

If you answered mostly "Yes": You might want to work on your ownership skills. At this rate you won't know which college you're attending until you get there!

If you answered mostly "No": You SO own your college application . . . and probably a lot of other stuff too!

56

Friends help friends get into college.

You and your best friend know each other inside and out. There's nobody better to keep each other in check when it comes to the college admissions process.

You're probably already study buddies; why not become admissions buddies too?

Together, you and your buddy can:

Push each other to maintain excellent grades.

Make studying for those scary standardized tests fun!

Develop college lists—after all, who knows where you would fit in better than your best friend?

And:

Stay on track with application deadlines.

Proofread and critique personal statements.

Road trip to college campuses with you.

Beg for teacher recommendations.

Talk each other down when things get stressful.

Only one qualification

Make sure your admissions buddy has the same drive for college as you do. You don't want to spend so much time pushing your best friend to do better at the expense of your own college dreams.

Would you give yourself some credit, already?

It seems as though you have to be almost superhuman if you want to get into college these days. With all that I've-got to-be-perfect pressure going on around you, it's easy to forget to tell yourself "Hey, nice job!"

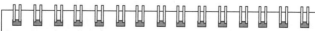

Hey, nice job!

- You are putting your all into this college application stuff—on top of all your other responsibilities—and that's not easy!
- Your schedule is as tight as J. Lo's jeans and you're **STILL** on target.
- You are keeping your grades up, staying committed to your extracurricular activities, communicating with your parents about college, taking exams, pouring your soul out onto applications . . . all while maintaining a cheery disposition (well, most of the time, anyway).
- You are an awesome college applicant. The admissions folks would be crazy not to notice that!

A little ME time?

Spend a day NOT thinking about college—
you deserve it!

Go bike riding with friends.

Do a little yoga.

Take a long relaxing bath.

Read a trashy novel that has no educational value whatsoever.

Park it in front of the Xbox for an entire afternoon.

Watch an all-day *Newlyweds* marathon on MTV.

Go through old family photos and collect some special ones to bring with you to college.

It doesn't matter what it is, as long as it's for you.

58 It's great to delegate!

You've got a laundry list of pre-college stuff that needs to get done—on top of keeping up with your grades, extracurricular activities, and everything else high school life has to offer. Handing over a few small tasks to your parents, if they're interested, keeps them involved, while leaving you more time to take on the rest.

Mom and Dad on assignment

You can ask them to do such tasks as:

- help keep track of application deadlines
- plan college tours around your schedule
- investigate financial aid options
- help you gather information about academic programs at your top choices
- proofread essays
- drive you to college fairs, tours, and to the mall to buy stuff for your dorm room

Only you can do it

Of course you have be hands on when it
comes to:

- deciding on your final list of colleges
- filling out college applications
- writing essays
- calling admissions offices
- setting up interviews
- getting recommendations
- writing thank you notes

Much too much

*If your parents are smothering you with
"help," talk to them. Explain that you
need quiet time to focus on your college
decisions and tasks. When you arrive at a
decision or complete a task, keep them in
the loop by updating them. You will
impress Mom and Dad (and yourself) by
being able to tackle the admissions process
and express yourself clearly.*

Take advantage of your high school guidance counselor's expertise.

*No, Mom wasn't wrong when she told you not to use people—**EXCEPT** when it comes to your counselor. That's what he/she's there for!*

Your counselor will help you

1. Discover where your interests and talents lie.

Plan a high school career full of fun and challenging coursework. **2.**

Keep on track with standardized tests and college applications. **3.**

4. Assist you with finding the right college as well as scholarships and financial aid.

5. Serve as a contact for colleges.

6. Write your Secondary School Report.

7. And more!

Take the first step

Find out who your assigned counselor is and introduce yourself. If you feel a little uncomfortable going into an unfamiliar person's office to say hi, you might want to:

1. *Smile!*
2. *Prepare what you want to talk about, so you have something to say after the initial "Hi, my name is Joe Student."*
3. *Bring a friend along for moral support (but go into the guidance counselor's office alone—if you are ready to apply to college, you should be able to talk to your guidance counselor all by yourself).*

Questions to ask your guidance counselor

1. By what date do you want to receive the list of colleges I'd like to apply to?
2. These are the colleges I'm considering—do you think they are good matches for me?
3. Are there any other colleges you would recommend?
4. What information do you need from me for my applications?
5. What is the high school's process for requesting letters of recommendation from teachers?
6. How much time do you need to process your letter of recommendation and the transcript?
7. Would you like a copy of my resume?
8. Do you know of any scholarships I might be eligible for?
9. Do you prefer to send out the entire application in one packet, or should I plan to send out my applications?
10. May I please have a copy of my official transcript to take along on college visits?

Your guidance counselor might be totally awesome . . . or be extremely busy...or both.

Most likely, your counselor will be friendly, accessible, and ready to help, but sometimes that's not quite the case. Usually this has to do with the amount of students a counselor has to deal with. Twenty is probably manageable but how about two hundred? It's tough enough to remember two hundred names, let alone individual personalities and college needs.

What if your counselor is overloaded?

Ever hear of the expression "the squeaky wheel gets the grease?" Well, there's a reason clichés exist . . . they're true! Visit your counselor's office often so that he or she can put a face to your name and get to know you.

What if your counselor doesn't even know your name?

If he or she doesn't know your name by your third visit, take these preventative measures:

- Begin the college process early.

- Ask a lot of questions. Don't wait for your counselor to offer information.

- Hand in your materials in September or October when your counselor is not swamped with work.

- Check back to make sure all of your materials were sent out.

It's **YOUR** life

Remember, even the greatest counselors are human and can make mistakes. When it comes right down to it, it's up to you to stay on top of opportunities and deadlines as well as your future.

61

Need more help? Consider asking an independent consultant for a second opinion.

An independent consultant does a job similar to your guidance counselor—for a fee.

The **pros**

- They will give you major attention and individualized college advice in a comfortable, informal setting and during flexible hours.
- Some consultants offer test-prep services in addition to counseling.
- Some specialize in opportunities for students with learning disabilities, student athletes, students considering medial school, students with less than stellar test scores, etc.
- They offer guidance through every step of the application process and insider info about how colleges will view your application.

The **cons**

- They don't have a day-to-day perspective on how you act in a class environment.
- It costs money. The fee can vary from a hundred bucks to a few thousand.
- Qualifications vary a **LOT**. Research and get references before you hire one.

Buyer beware!

It is an unethical (and illegal) practice for a consultant to promise acceptance to a particular school or to write a college essay for you. If a consultant offers you either of these things, run!

It's not only WHAT you know. . . .

WHO you know is important, too. If you have questions about a college's particular requirements, then get to know the admissions department!

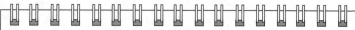

People to talk to

<u>Admissions reps:</u> Ask them about requirements and deadlines. Set up a campus visit or even an interview with the folks who say yea or nay to your application.

<u>Financial aid folks:</u> Find out about available loan programs as well as the scholarships and grants they offer, if any.

<u>Career services people:</u> Question them about working in your field of interest: starting salaries, employment demand, reputation of an intended program in the business world, etc. Inquire about students with similar career goals and their success stories, too.

The deal

Most colleges read applications by region. Each region is assigned to a specific admissions person, who is usually the "first read" on your application. This regional officer will usually present your file to the admissions board, and may or may not advocate for your acceptance to the college. It's important to know who "your" regional officer is, as this person can be a powerful influence in your admission. Stay in touch with him or her throughout the college process by email, note, or phone. Update the officer if you've won another award, increased your G.P.A. or test scores, or had a unique experience.

MYTH:

"If I call the college too much, I'll become annoying to the staff."

MYTHBUSTER:

True, if you're calling just to chat. Not true if you're calling for a legitimate purpose. In fact, most colleges record how many times a student contacts their college because it shows you're interested. So, calling might actually HELP your chances!

Schmooze it or lose it.

It's a fact of life. People are more inclined to lend a hand to those they know and like before they'd aid a stranger. And when it comes to college admissions, students need all the help they can get!

What is schmoozing?

It's all about forming a network of people who can possibly help you someday—or at least connect you with someone who can. Schmoozing might gain you access to stuff such as: inside info on college requirements, a possible interview at a selective college, or maybe even a scholarship!

How to schmooze

1. **Get out there:** Be an active member in your church or other community organization.

2. **Be friendly:** Talk to as many people as possible.

3. **Be helpful:** If you can make someone's life easier, do it. It could be as simple as setting up a phone call between your brother who attends Purdue and the head cheerleader who wants to go there.

4. **Let them know what your goals are:** Whether it's a rewarding summer job, a possible scholarship, or just a date for the prom. You never know who can help.

5. **Say thank you:** Mom's right—when someone helps you out, make sure to take the time to write a thank you note. It will be appreciated, and it will encourage that person to support you in the future.

5. **Return the favor:** Like any relationship, it's got to work both ways.

Who to schmooze

- family, family friends, friends, and friends' families
- church members and community organizations
- teachers, counselors, and coaches
- your boss, other business owners, and professional groups
- the bus driver, the people sitting on the blanket next to you at the park, whoever!

64 Talk to your high school's alumni.

Everyone remembers their high school days, and the bond you have with alumni from your high school gives you an edge. Get the scoop on college from people who have been though it . . . and survived.

Been there, done that

If you don't know any recent grads from your school, ask your guidance counselor to put you in touch with a few who are attending colleges on your wish list.

How come you need to talk to recent grads?

Because you'll get insider info on the colleges of your choice. Ask them about classes, life on and off campus, college activities, etc.

Because they'll tell you what worked for them and what didn't. Ask them about their personal statement, the interview process, scholarships, grants, etc.

Because you'll get to hear inspiring real-life stories. Ask them how it is to live with a roommate, how college is different from high school, if it's everything they thought it would be, etc.

The gray guys . . .

Don't forget to speak with older alums too. They're an important and often forgotten resource. Here are just a few ways they can help:

- *If in business, he or she might give you a part-time job.*

- *Perhaps one works for a major company that can hook you up with a major scholarship.*

- *An alumnus might be an influential member on a college review board who can put in a good word for you. You never know!*

Find a mentor.

Guidance, something to aspire toward, and perspective from an adult who isn't related to you . . . those are just a few of the many things you will gain from a mentor.

Mentor match up

Finding a mentor usually comes naturally. It could be your favorite teacher or coach, the owner of a trendy café, your volunteer coordinator, an older and successful student, or a family friend that you admire. It doesn't really matter WHO it is—just as long as he or she is a positive influence on your life. If you're having trouble finding a mentor, talk to a teacher or guidance counselor about tutoring or mentoring programs in your high school or community.

Take your mentor to lunch day

Why not? As she is picking on a slice of pizza, you can be picking her brain. (Ask her to tell you her life story.) How did she get to be the person she is today? What kind of dreams did she have when she was your age? Having a role model is informative, fun, and can build your confidence about the choice YOU are making for YOUR life!

Uncle Sam wants a relationship with . . . you!

A give and take relationship with Uncle Sam will definitely help achieve your college goals. The catch? In order to receive aid, you must give a commitment to the armed forces.

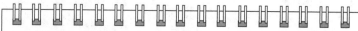

Before college options

- Check out the pros and cons of enlisting in the Army, Navy, Air Force, or Marines. After your tour is over, you can take advantage of the GI Bill, which contributes to an education fund.

- Find out if your parents were ever part of the military. If so, you might be eligible for help with a loan.

During college options

- Attend a military academy for "free." After college, you'll serve four years in the military as an officer. Be aware, though, that admission to a military academy is extremely competitive and requires superior grades, activities, and test scores, as well as a letter of recommendation from a Senator, State Representative, or ranking government official.

- Learn about Coast Guard, National Guard, or Reserves scholarship opportunities and/or part-time service.

After college options

- Need help with a hefty student loan? Uncle Sam will lend you a hand—even if you join up after college.

Part
Four:

Steps to the
Perfect
Application

67 Start the application process early.

Students, teachers, and guidance counselors all say the same thing: The earlier, the better.

3 reasons to start early

1. You'll be less likely to make mistakes on the application or forget to send requested materials.

You'll have more time to turn your personal statement into a work of art. **2.**

3. You'll be less stressed and more able to enjoy senior year!

3 ways to start early

(1.)

Mark a calendar with all of your college deadlines so you don't forget them.

(2.) **Set up a checklist for: writing the first draft of your essay, requesting recommendations, and official high school transcripts, etc.**

(3.) **Dedicate specific times to work on your application—and stick to it!**

Reward yourself

Avoid falling into the procrastination trap by rewarding yourself with something fun after each completed task: shopping at the mall, an ice cream sundae splurge, or a day at the beach with your buds, whatever!

68

Go get your applications.

By now, you've weeded through the tons of college admissions stuff that you picked up at college fairs and received in the mail. What remains (in a perfect pile of organization, of course) are the brochures and applications you need to apply to your top choices. Right?

Oops

- If you find that you don't have an application that you need, go to the college's website and click on their undergraduate admissions requirements to find out if they accept online applications. If you do apply online, remember to print out proof of submission!

- Most colleges offer downloadable applications on their websites. Download away! (Just make sure you have ALL components of each application.) If you are unclear about what you need, call the admissions office—they'll be glad to help a prospective student!

- If you are unable to apply online or download applications, go to your high school's guidance office to see if they have any "extra" applications lying around. (Remember the ones you donated? Hopefully others have done the same...)
- You can always call a college's admissions office to request that they send you application materials through the mail.

While you're at it

- Stock up on mailing supplies like large envelopes, binder clips, and stamps to use when sending in your applications.
- Figure out where you will make copies of everything before you send it.
- What are you doing on the days each application is due? Make sure you can get to the post office before it closes in case you, ahem, are running a bit late and are submitting applications on the actual due dates. But of course, you'll be so ahead of the game that you won't have to worry about it—right?

TIP

69

Make yourself a "brag sheet" (i.e., activity resume).

Now's not the time to be modest. Include all your awesome accomplishments with your college applications. How else is anybody supposed to know how fabulous you are?

Show your stuff

Create an activity resume listing all of your accomplishments and activities, such as

- Volunteer work
- Activities (both in and out of school activities)
  - Athletics
  - Honors and awards
    - Employment
  - Other accomplishments

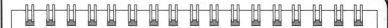

Tips for a stellar activity resume

1. List your most impressive and important activities first.

2. Highlight specific details about your activities.

3. Use active verbs to describe your roles, i.e., assisted, starred, led, participated, completed, performed, etc.

4. Keep the page neat, organized and easy to read. Ask for help with formatting if you need it.

5. Spell out acronyms. Admissions officers don't know that WHSSC stands for Westborough High School Science Club.

Share your stuff

Give your resume to teachers/counselors who are writing recommendation letters for you. It'll help them get a full handle on your accomplishments.

Hand it to admissions counselors at the start of your interviews so they can ask you questions about your achievements.

Send it along with every application.

70 Create a "professional" email address, and dedicate it to college-related correspondence.

*Come on, now. Do you **REALLY** want to send applications to college admissions officers— the very people you are trying to impress— from your **sugarlips@2cute.com** email address?*

Uh, didn't think so.

Do it!

Drop this book right now and register for a new and improved email address with a formal ID such as: **joestudent@yahoo.com** or **Jstudent18@netscape.com**, etc. Most browsers will give you an email account for free. All you have to do is set it up!

Don't even think about it . . .

*Your friends might think an ID like "punkrockfanatic"
is cute; but admissions officers might be apt to
disagree.*

Free = good

Check out Yahoo, MSN, and
Gmail (Google), for free email
accounts. You may even want to
create a specific account for
your college application process
so you can keep all of your
correspondence with admissions
departments and references
organized. Use this email address
on applications, at college fairs,
on admissions and scholarship
websites—anything related to
your college search.

TIP

71

A strong concept is the first step to a strong personal statement.

You will have to write a strong personal statement (essay) to get into college, as well as any supplemental essays required by your college picks.

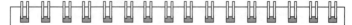

Say *no* to writer's block

- Start thinking about the essays early, preferably the summer between junior and senior year (maybe even sooner if you are going for early decision or early action applications).

- Reflect on what makes you unique: what you do and why and how you do it.

- Carry a small notepad with you to jot down sudden revelations.

- Read. Sometimes an inspiring book can motivate an excellent essay.

- Go through old photos to jog memories of meaningful events.

Be careful!

If you have to write more than one essay, you might find yourself wanting to "tweak" your personal statement again and again to fit each college's requirement. If this is the case, proofreading is KEY! You don't want to mention how attending Lehigh University is essential for your human development if you're applying to Penn State. Also, keep in mind that admissions officers can spot a lightly altered essay right away and may be offended by a student who didn't take the time to answer their essay questions properly.

The Common Application (CA)

The CA is a general application form used by over 150 independent colleges. If your prospective colleges accept the CA, you will have to write the major essay/personal statement, the supplemental essay required by each college, AND a short essay on what your favorite activity is and why. Ask your guidance counselor for the form or get one online at **commonapp.org**.

Think your essay has to be the most polished and perfect piece of writing ever? Think again!

The admissions folks aren't looking for Shakespeare, they want to hear from the REAL you. Show them your unique qualities and accomplishments.

5 tips to an excellent essay

1.

Write it yourself. It's okay to have someone make suggestions on how to improve your essay, but in the end, the writing has to be all you, baby.

2. <u>Use your own voice.</u> Grammar is important, but admissions officers don't expect your prose to be super sophisticated **BEFORE** you're admitted to their colleges—only after you graduate.

3. <u>Be an individual.</u> Don't write what you **THINK** they want to hear. What are you, psychic? Besides, admissions offices can get pretty bored reading the same tired essay topic over and over.

4. <u>Think small.</u> That's right. Narrow down your statement from say, how we can achieve world peace, to something like, how you used diplomacy to stop your little brother from throwing water balloons at your dates.

5. <u>Make it personal.</u> Reveal some kind of personal growth, deeply held value, or unique interest by focusing on a particular event in your life. You can write about the moment you realized you wanted to be a doctor, the lessons you learned at a job or internship, a relationship that changed your life, or any topic that demonstrates insight and growth.

Avoid personal statement traps.

There's no such thing as a perfect personal statement, but you can avoid some dangerous traps—if you know what they are.

Make no mistake

1. *Don't write a boring first sentence.* College admissions officers pour through thousands of essays, and they'll be more likely to read past the first sentence of yours if it's an attention-grabber.

2. *Don't focus on others.* Colleges want to learn about YOU. Unless you are specifically asked to write about someone else, don't.

3. *Don't use clichés.* Nothing makes an essay reader more frustrated than having to read the same expression over and over.

4. *Don't get weird in order to seem creative.* You do want to take a creative approach to an essay topic, but you don't want to cross the line into bizarre.

5. *Don't use flowery, artificial language.* It just says, "trying too hard."

6. *Don't procrastinate.* Waiting until the last minute is a surefire way to sabotage a powerful essay.

7. *Don't whine.* Nobody wants to hear someone complain.

8. *Don't restate your resume.* A laundry list of extracurricular activities does not offer interesting insights into your life and dreams.

9. *Don't be repetitive.* Communicate your points once and well.

10. *Don't plagiarize.* The admissions people know about all the college essay websites and books that have tons of essays. You will most likely get caught—as well as rejected.

74

You never know what could make an admissions officer banish your application to the reject pile.

10 pet peeves of college admissions officers

1. Late applications.
2. Sloppy/illegible handwriting—how can they evaluate something if they can't read it?
3. Incomplete applications or forgetting to forward high school transcripts.
4. Plagiarism.
5. Endless essays. Straying a bit from the word count is okay, but a 10-page essay is a definite no-no.
6. Typos and grammatical errors.
7. Florescent paper or other obvious attempts "to stand out."
8. Using pencil or red or scented ink.
9. Too many recommendation letters—two or three are sufficient; 20 is going overboard.
10. Unsolicited videotapes and other media products when there's no time to view them.

Things that make admissions officers smile

- *Students who follow directions— sending only **requested** materials and answering each essay question to the best of their ability.*

- *An application with personality— they want to feel as though they know you after they've read it.*

- *Glowing and personalized letters of recommendation.*

- *Essays that reflect a student's passions, interests, or personality.*

- *Students who know **why** they want to attend a particular college—and it's not just because it has a "big name."*

- *Follow-up calls to ensure that all application materials have arrived.*

- *Thank-you letters.*

Consider applying early decision.

You know that rumor about students gaining an edge by applying to a college early decision? It's true! Early decision means you apply in the fall and hear the good news by winter break. Colleges tend to accept more early decision applicants because the students who apply under early decision programs are usually of exceptionally high quality and are certain to attend. That's because they have to . . . or ELSE!

Pressure to decide

Consider the following questions before you send in an early decision application:

> Do I **REALLY** want to go to this college? If accepted, you are bound to attend and cannot change your mind.

Do I want to apply to other colleges too? You're not allowed to if you're applying early decision.

Do I fit the academic profile of the college? If not, then early decision probably won't help your chances of getting in.

Am I ready to apply to OTHER colleges if I'm NOT accepted under early decision? If you are not accepted under early decision, you will automatically be considered as a regular decision applicant. That you selected to apply to a college under early decision shows a sincere interest in the college, so you may get "brownie points" during the regular application review, but remember, you are NOT guaranteed a spot, so you should apply to other colleges just in case.

Consider applying early action.

Want the benefit of early decision without the pressure of a decision? You can have your cake and eat it too!

Acting early

<u>Early Action:</u> You apply early but, unlike early decision, you don't have to sign an agreement promising that you'll attend. Also, you're free to apply early action to as many colleges as you want to. You'll get word by winter break if you're in—and you don't have to tell them if you're attending until May.

<u>Single-Choice Early Action:</u> This new option is offered by some colleges in lieu of plain old early action. The difference? You can only file one S.C.E.A. application, but you can apply to as many colleges as you want under regular admission. It's a good choice if you want to apply to a college early but also want the option of comparing financial aid packages—something you can't do with early decision.

Early decision vs. early action: The Quiz

1. I've completed all my college visitations and research before I begin my senior year.

   ___ yes ___ no

2. Only ONE college stands out as the perfect match for me.

   ___ yes ___ no

3. I meet or exceed the academic profile of my first-choice college.

   ___ yes ___ no

4. I've challenged myself academically, and my grades have been consistent.

   ___ yes ___ no

5. My parents and I feel that I do not need to compare financial aid packages.

   ___ yes ___ no

6. I've completed my essay(s) and have assembled a list of all my activities before senior year begins.

   ___ yes ___ no

7. My ACT or SAT score meets or exceeds the average score of incoming applicants

   ___ yes ___ no

Early decision vs. early action: The analysis

1-3 yes responses: You're on the right track in your college search, but you're probably not ready for early decision. Maybe a nonbinding early action will work for you.

4-6 yes responses: You might want to consider early decision, but consult with your parents and guidance counselor to make sure.

7 yes responses: You seem to have all your bases covered and are a strong candidate for early decision. Consult your parents and counselor before you apply.

Send in applications as soon as possible after first quarter grades appear on your transcript.

Not all colleges wait until after their "official" due dates to review general admissions applications. In fact, many don't. So, even if you're not participating in early decision or early action, you should submit yours as early as you can.

Application Tip

Get TWO application packets from each college. Fill out one application for each college, then ask Mom or Dad or your guidance counselor to review them. When you get feedback, fill out the second application—that way, your applications will be perfect in every way!

The process

Well before the due date, admissions officers may conduct a "first read." During this process, students are divided into *yes, no,* and *maybe* piles. The *yes* students are likely to be admitted, the *no* students are likely to be rejected, and the *maybe* students will be considered again in comparison to the rest of the applicant pool as those applications come in closer to the due date. So, if you happen to be a maybe, applying early may not affect your chances. But for all you YESes out there, it definitely will!

The earlier you deliver an application, the...

...more time your high school guidance office has to complete their submissions...

... less exhausted the application review committee will be, so your application will get an energetic look-see...

...more time the committee has to ensure all of your materials have been received...

...more impressive you look, because you are such an organized go-getter!

Sending in your applications on time is NOT enough. You need proof that you did it!

Applications can get lost in the mail—or even by admissions departments—and it'll be your tough luck if you can't prove that you met deadlines.

Via email

If you're sending your applications electronically, make sure you save a copy of this important email in your "Sent" folder. Wait a week, then call the colleges to find out if they received your application.

Via snail mail

If you're sending your applications the old fashioned way, spring for the extra bucks and send each one "Certified Return Receipt Requested." You'll get postcards in the mail stating when the applications were received and who signed for it. If you don't, call the post office (or go online) to trace them.

Keep copies of everything!

Just in case your application IS lost,
you'll be able to send another one ASAP.

Make a follow-up call

A week or two after you send in your application, call the college to verify that they have received it and to check that they have all of the materials required to complete your file (including transcripts, letters of recommendation, test scores, etc.). Always wait a week or two so they have time to process your file—just think of the tons of mail that an admissions office receives! And remember: The bigger the college, the bigger the piles of applications, and the bigger chance they won't get through them as quickly.

If you are delivering your applications online, remember to ask your guidance counselor to forward your transcript and letters of recommendation, too!

Forgetting to do so is a common mistake among students. Don't let it happen to you!

Good to know

1. Colleges must receive proof of your sparkling 4.0 G.P.A. in writing.

2. You can't just give them a copy of your report card. You must request that your high school send them an official transcript directly.

3. Don't expect your high school to forward your transcript overnight—especially if you go to a large school. Request it early.

Little reminders

Keep forgetting to ask the office to send out your transcript? Try these little reminders:

1. Scatter reminder stickies on your bedroom mirror, your backpack, the fridge, the windshield of your car, etc.
2. Tie ribbons to your pinkie in your favorite college colors to jog your memory.
3. LAST RESORT! Ask your mom to send you a text message during your lunch period to remind you to do it then.

Forgetting $omething?

Did you pay your application fee online? No? Well, remember to **SEND YOUR CHECK** *to the college! Yes? Print out the confirmation for proof of payment!*

TIP

80

There's still hope if you miss the application deadline.

You DON'T want to miss a deadline, but there are a few options out there if you do.

Try this

Try contacting the colleges. If they haven't already received tons of applications, you might be able to convince them to take yours late. If so, you'd better be ready to hand in your stuff ASAP.

Check out colleges that have rolling admission. They may be all booked, but it can't hurt to look. You can find out which colleges offer rolling admission by visiting a college search engine such as **collegeboard.com** or **fastweb.com**.

Go to the NACAC website.
The National Association
for College Admission Counseling publishes
a Space Availability Survey in late May.
Visit **nacac.com** often for updates.

Think about community college. Depending
on how much room is available, you may be
able to enroll as late as the first week of
classes.

Research colleges that offer January
admissions. And make sure you don't
miss THIS deadline!

Gentle reminder

*If you maintain organized files and schedule your
application process carefully, you won't be late!*

The more a college wants you, the more likely they are to offer a financial aid package containing higher amounts of scholarship money and less loan money.

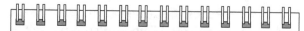

Financial aid is available in several forms:

- Scholarships (free money based on grades)
- Grants (free money based on need and/or grades)
- Loans (private or federal, you've got to pay them back eventually)
- Work Study Programs (work off part of your tuition through an on-campus job)

Show me the (free) money!

If financial aid is extremely important to your family, you might want to think about applying to colleges that are just below your academic profile. This way you'll be a more desirable candidate, and you will be more likely to receive significant scholarship and grant aid— the kind you don't have to pay back!

Financial aid worksheet

Talk to your guidance counselor about creating a chart that identifies the average financial aid given by each college, the forms required by each, and the deadlines for each form. This will help you and your family keep track of your financial aid applications. Just like your other applications, financial aid apps can get lost in the mail—remember to keep copies of all the documents you submit!

82 Apply for financial aid—even if you think you won't get any.

When it comes to financial aid, guidance counselors say that the biggest mistakes families make are applying too late or not applying at all.

You've got to be in it to win it

Fill out the FAFSA (Free Application for Federal Student Aid). Pick one up from your guidance office (in November of your senior year), or check out **fafsa.ed.gov** for a copy of the form.

Some colleges may require that you submit the CSS (College Scholarship Profile) as well as a FAFSA. You can find this form in your guidance office or at **profileonline.collegeboard.com**. The CSS provides more detailed information about your family's financial status, which allows private colleges to evaluate other factors in your request for financial aid.

Earlier is always better

Colleges tend to be more generous with the first few financial aid packages awarded than the last few. Ask your parents to file their taxes in January instead of April. This way you can send in the FAFSA way earlier than the rest of the financial aid seekers, and you'll have a good shot at a better package.

For the boys

If you're a guy, make sure you register for the Selective Service by your 18th birthday. Otherwise you won't be eligible for federal aid. You can register on your FAFSA form or go to the Selective Service website at **sss.gov**.

You don't have to take the first financial aid package that comes along.

Try it

Excellent students often have colleges competing for their enrollment. If you don't think the financial aid package at your top choice is good enough, call them and respectfully let them know what the other colleges are offering. Your top choice just might meet the best plan.

Even if you're not the best student out there, you still have a chance to improve an aid package if you can provide information about changed financial circumstances such as a lost job or a medical expense that was not included on your forms.

Schedule an appointment
with a financial aid officer at
your first-choice college, and
tell them how much you need
to attend.

Ask about work study programs; if a
college knows you are willing to work
there to attend, they may revisit the
work study budget and reallocate some
to you.

What the financial aid folks won't tell you . . .

*Want to know a very early (and easy) way to
squeeze free money out of a college? Ask the
admissions office for a financial aid pre-read.
They can project what they will be able to give
you before you even apply. In many cases, if
similar colleges have vastly different packages,
they will attempt to match their offers!*
(Ivy Alert: the Ivies **DO NOT** *conduct
pre-reads.)*

Would you believe that saving for college might not be right for everyone?

Let's face it. The piggybank your parents bought when you were six isn't big enough to hold your college tuition, and the 529 and Coverdell college-savings plans are so confusing, your best bet is to figure them out before you jump in.

The plans explained . . .

Basically, the 529 and Coverdell are educational investments in which parents invest in one of many state-run mutual funds without having to pay taxes on returns or withdrawals—as long as the money is spent on college.

Be aware

- Trudging through the multitude of paperwork and fees can be a daunting task. Your parents might want to seek professional help to select the right one for the family.

- Saving for college in a 529 or Coverdell plan could somewhat reduce your financial aid package, as will sizable income and assets.

- If you end up winning a full scholarship (or receiving a significant inheritance or other sum of money) and don't need the money in your college savings plan, then your parents are going to get an ENORMOUS tax penalty.

Don't do it yourself!

You should **NOT** set up personal savings accounts in your own name. Financial aid folks expect students to contribute a more significant percentage of their income and assets to college than they expect from parents.

85

Sometimes financial aid packages just don't cut it. You might need a backup plan.

More than half of college students get some kind of financial aid, and more than half of the aid comes in the form of loans.

Federal loans

Stafford and Perkins loans are offered to qualifying students at low interest rates but limit borrowing from about $2,500 to $5,500 per year (not much if you want to attend a private college).

Options, options

You might want to consider . . .

- Taking out a private loan at a higher interest rate in addition to your federal loan.
- Appealing to the financial aid folks at your top choice. Sometimes colleges will reconsider their offer if they know you're going to attend the college.
- Attending the college that offers the best financial aid package.

Net worth

Sometimes a high-priced college is worth going to, sometimes it isn't. Make a list of the pros and cons to find out if your college experience will outweigh the debt you may incur.

TIP

86

All scholarships are NOT created equal.

Most scholarships offered to budding college students are on the up and up, but some are created for the sole purpose of separating you from your money.

Learn some signs of scholarship scams

There are no guidelines. Whether you're the first person in your family to attend college or you wrote the most awesome essay on your love for Swiss cheese, there is always a reason for a scholarship. No legitimate scholarship fund will offer you money for nothing.

You're told that you will definitely receive money. A scholarship cannot legitimately promise that you will win anything in advance.

There is an application fee. You shouldn't have to pay even $1 to apply for a scholarship.

You're asked to supply personal information. Under no circumstances should you provide your social security number or bank account numbers in order to receive a scholarship.

Weird scholarships aren't necessarily scams

For instance, the legitimate "Stuck-at-Prom" scholarship contest rewards high school students who wear duct tape to their Prom! The moral? Check out the program before you apply for the cash. Most scholarships from groups like this are for one year only—don't forget to renew each year!

Letters of recommendation aren't the top factor in admissions, but they **CAN** make or break your application.

An excellent letter may catch an admissions officer's eye, while a scathing one can ensure a student's denial.

Recommendation Checklist

Find out if any of the colleges you will be applying to require a recommendation from a teacher in a specific subject area. Most colleges require three letters of reference: one from a principal or guidance counselor and two from academic teachers (sorry, no gym or health teachers) who have taught you in the last few years. Do not submit additional letters unless requested by the college.

☐ Try to acquire references from different parts of your life. People who know different things about you will draw a more complete picture of you.

☐ Choose references who can talk about your academic progress and your desire to achieve success.

☐ Carefully select those who will write on your behalf so that you feel secure about the content of the recommendations.

To view or not to view

Waiving your right to read a recommendation before it is sent out may add value to the opinion, but do so only if you are positive that the letter will be written to your benefit. If you have carefully chosen your references, you should have full confidence waiving your right to see your letters. Recommenders will be more cautious if you do not waive the right to view them, and colleges will wonder what you have to hide…

There's a right way and a wrong way to acquire recommendations.

The right way

- Get recommendations from teachers who **KNOW** you well and who can **WRITE** well. A glowing review from your favorite math guru doesn't pack a punch if he can't put a sentence together.

- Make sure your references are relevant. If you want to major in marine biology, it might be best to ask a science or math teacher to write one.

- Ask early—and give your recommender at least two weeks to write it. If you know for sure who you want to ask, start dropping hints at the end of junior year...they may want to write your letter during summer break!

- Create a "cheat sheet" to help teachers write about you. List accomplishments, goals, and the colleges you'd like to attend. Give it (and your activity resume) to your recommender before he/she writes your letter.

- Send thank-you notes! The handwritten kind; not a mass email.

The wrong way

- Don't ask the popular teacher who doesn't know you very well.
- Don't wait until the last minute to ask and then expect it done ASAP.
- Don't pressure a teacher to write one when it's clear they don't want to do it.
- Don't forget to thank your recommenders.

Sell yourself.

Admissions officers use personal interviews to get to know you and to gauge your level of interest in the college.

Don't stress over interviews!

Most interviews last between 20-40 minutes and go a little something like this:

- An intro and a handshake
- A little small talk
- A conversation about the college and/or some programs
- A discussion about your academic accomplishments, interests, and goals
- An opportunity for you to ask questions
- A thank you and a handshake

Top Interview Advice from the Guidance Gurus

1. Run through a mock interview with your guidance counselor or someone you know.

2. If you are confident about your interviewing skills, schedule an interview with your number one choice first. Otherwise, you may want to "practice" on your second- or third-choice college before hitting number one.

3. Research the college ahead of time so you can speak intelligently about programs that interest you.

4. Show up on time and dress appropriately (casual, but neat).

5. Talk to the interviewer alone—ask your parents to wait for you outside.

6. Be yourself . . . but use language that you would with your grandma, not your pals.

7. Know WHY you want to attend the college.

8. Stress academics first and activities second—admissions folks want to see you as an academically motivated student.

9. Anticipate a few questions the interviewer might ask as well as your answer. But don't practice so much that you sound fake.

10. Be prepared to ask a few meaningful questions—ones that can't be answered in the college catalog or on their website.

11. Relax! Remember, you're interviewing THEM as much as they're interviewing you.

Avoid using filler words such as "uh," "like," and "you know?" in college interviews.

Because, like, admissions officers think it, uh, makes a really smart student sound, like, totally stupid—you know?

So, like, why do you do it?

- 'Cause you're nervous! Duh, everybody is!
- 'Cause you're trying to think of something brilliant to say and you need something to fill up the silence until it comes to you.
- 'Cause it's a bad habit you developed in third grade, and now you have no idea you're even doing it.

The 3-Step de-"like"-ing program

1. Take a day to really focus on what you're saying. You might be surprised at, like, what comes out of your mouth every few seconds.

Think of some tough questions a college admissions officer might ask, and practice answering into a tape recorder. See how you sound. Keep it up until the filler words stop spewing. **2.**

3. Contribute a dollar to a "Filler Fund" every time you say the word "like." Make a game out of it with friends and have them do the same. By the end of the week, you all should be speaking like interview pros. If not, at least you'll have money to throw a pizza party.

If you feel an "um" coming on, pause and take a deep breath— it will make you look thoughtful, instead of grasping.

Watch out for interview curveballs.

College admissions officers might throw you a curveball to see how you'll react in the interview. Be prepared!

10 tricky questions they've asked in the past
How would YOU handle them?

1. What was the worst decision you've ever made?
2. How would your friends characterize you?
3. What is your biggest regret about high school, and if you could change it, what impact would it have on you and in your future as a college student?
4. If you were a world leader, what would you do to heal the violence and turbulence in the world?
5. How do you see yourself 20 years from now?
6. Who is the most influential person in your life and how?
7. What are you reading right now?
8. What makes you qualified to attend this college?
9. What will be your greatest challenge in college?
10. What separates this university from others?

One more for good luck . . .
(Some say it's the toughest question of them all.)

11. Do you have any questions?

Part Five:

Ten Things to Remember Once You Get In

Don't forget to say "thanks" AND "no thanks."

It's the least you can do, and it's often forgotten. So break out the pen and paper and send a little note . . . it'll go a long way.

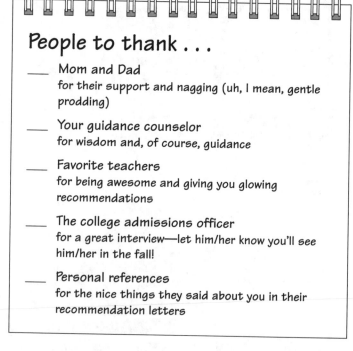

People to thank . . .

___ **Mom and Dad**
for their support and nagging (uh, I mean, gentle prodding)

___ **Your guidance counselor**
for wisdom and, of course, guidance

___ **Favorite teachers**
for being awesome and giving you glowing recommendations

___ **The college admissions officer**
for a great interview—let him/her know you'll see him/her in the fall!

___ **Personal references**
for the nice things they said about you in their recommendation letters

Sample thank-you note

Dear Mr. Gonzalez,

Thank you for all of your help with my college applications. You really helped me organize my search and assemble my applications—I couldn't have done it without you. I'll let you know when the acceptance letters start rolling in!

Thanks again.

Sincerely,
Joe Student

Thanks but no thanks . . .

After making your final college choice, don't forget to tell the other institutions that you WON'T be attending. You don't want them to hold a place that could be filled by another student, right?

93

Make new friends at freshman orientation.

You'll be glad to have a few friendly faces to look up once your parents drop you off at your dorm room.

Freshman Orientation 101

For freshman only, of course, it's a time (usually a few weeks before classes begin) to get a feel for the campus and to meet others in your graduating class.

What will you do?

Learn how to get around campus.

Stay in the dorm with roommates for a couple of nights.

Participate in fun "freshman bonding" activities.

Register for your first classes.

Make the most of it

* Be friendly and TALK to people.
* Join a game of Frisbee or Hacky Sack or start your own.
* Hang out with your orientation roomies and the other kids on your floor.
* Go over the course catalog, and make a list of classes that you'd like to take.
* Make sure you have alternates when you go to register. Being a freshman, you may not get your first choices (or your second ones).
* Find your classrooms, the laundry room, and the cafeteria.
* Explore the area around campus—check out shopping, restaurants, and the landscape where you'll be spending the next four years.

Don't panic if you forget something.

Whether it's your favorite teddy bear or your funky new flip-flops, be forewarned, you WILL forget something.

Use this checklist to remember important stuff you'll need for dorm life.

☐ extra-long sheets (the regular ones won't fit the extra-long beds)

☐ blankets, quilts, and pillows

☐ towels and washcloths

☐ toiletries

☐ shower caddy (to carry your toiletries to the community bathroom)

☐ bathrobe

☐ desk lamp

☐ iron and ironing board

☐ alarm clock

☐ bulletin board, thumbtacks, stapler, tape, and sticky notes

- [ ] calendar

- [ ] posters and pictures for your walls

- [ ] pencils, pens, and highlighters

- [ ] extension cords, surge protectors, and batteries

- [ ] CD/DVD player, music, and movies

- [ ] full-length mirror

- [ ] clothes and hangers

- [ ] a few dishes, cups, and containers

- [ ] quarters and laundry supplies (including a hamper or laundry bag)

- [ ] pots and pans (if you're not enrolled in a meal plan)

- [ ] computer, printer, iPod, walkman, other electronics, and all the cables and chargers that go with them!

- [ ] camera

- [ ] _____

- [ ] _____

- [ ] _____

- [ ] _____

Contact your roommate(s) at least once before you head off to college.

Whether it's by phone or email, get acquainted so you'll know what to expect.

Questions, questions . . .

Stressing over what to say during that first phone call to your new roomie? You know, the total stranger you'll be living with? Here are a few conversation starters to get you past that awkward feeling:

1. Do you know what your major is?
2. What type of music are you into?
3. Are you an early bird or a night owl?
4. Do you have a boyfriend/girlfriend?
5. Are you thinking of joining any clubs on campus?

Fast friends?

If you hit it off right away, great! If not, don't worry about it. Most friendships take time to develop. And remember, you don't have to be best friends to share a room.

Roomie to-do's before move-in day

- Learn the layout of your room and what kind of furniture is provided so you'll know how big (or small) it is. This way you can figure out how much to bring.
- Find out what appliances your college prohibits. You don't want to lug a mini fridge all that way only to find your parents have to lug it back home.
- Do you and your roommate want to coordinate your decorating styles?
- Discuss what to share with your roommate so you don't double up: a telephone, TV, mini fridge, microwave, vacuum, radio, etc.

96

Reality check: Most college students are B-R-O-K-E!

*Guess what? Tuition does **NOT** cover everything. Sure, it's a big part of your expense, but it's the little things that can catch you off guard.*

In addition to tuition

Plan on spending your dough on . . .

___ Room and board. Check your college—some include this expense in the tuition cost, but some don't.

___ Other miscellaneous college fees. On-campus parking, course-related fees, student services, and health insurance can all incur fees.

___ Books and supplies. Don't be surprised if you find yourself paying hundreds of dollars for your Psych 101 textbook and the highlighters you'll need to mark important passages.

___ Personal items. You'll be forking over big bucks on toiletries, laundry stuff, clothes, phone bills, movies, trips home, midnight pizza runs, and more.

Deep discounts

___ Reduce book expenses significantly by buying gently used texts instead of brand, spankin' new ones.

___ You're a student now. Ask for student freebies and discounts at restaurants, movie theaters, museums, airlines, etc.

___ Consider getting a part-time job that offers an employee discount.

___ Explore free entertainment that you can do with your friends: concerts and athletics, working out at the college sports complex, hanging out in the quad, etc.

___ Opt for the college's meal plan—at least freshman year. Then dining will be one out-of-pocket expense you won't have to worry about.

___ Hang out on campus—most college activities are free or close to it!

Know your spending limits BEFORE you get into trouble.

It is SO easy to dig yourself into a big pit of debt. As if by magic, becoming a college freshman will suddenly make you an attractive credit card candidate, even though you have no way to pay the bills.

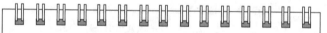

The good news

- It's the easiest way to form a credit history, which is really important nowadays.

- It's awesome if you're ever in an emergency and you're out of cash.

- If it gets stolen, you won't be responsible for illegal charges if you notify the credit card company ASAP.

- Hey, they might even give you a free T-shirt for applying!

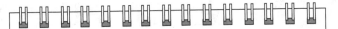

The bad news

- Charging stuff is, in essence, borrowing money. If you don't pay off that bill at the end of the month, you'll have to pay interest on the loan (probably at a hefty rate).
- If you miss a payment or two, your interest rate will skyrocket even more.
- If you keep charging and not paying, after four years you'll end up owing big on a student loan AND a credit card.
- Bad payment practices in college can ruin your credit history before it even begins.

Keep it in check

- *Search for a company that gives you a low interest rate or stuff like: frequent flyer miles, buyer protection, cash back, etc., and apply for the card with the best deal.*
- *Before charging, consider if you can pay the balance at the end of the month.*
- *If not, then ask yourself: Is this an emergency? If the answer is something like, "I'll DIE if I don't get these extra cheesy Nachos," don't charge it.*

98

Nobody's going to push you to do well in class— you have to push yourself.

Maybe your high school teachers pulled you aside if you slacked off in class, but this is college, baby. And there's no handholding in college.

5 ways to succeed in class

1. If available, seek assistance developing college skills. We're talking note taking, researching, writing, and managing your time. Most colleges offer tutoring and study skills workshops free of charge.

Show up for class, and do your work on time. Sounds simple enough, but if you slack off on either, you'll fall way behind in class. **2.**

3. Set up a daily study schedule—and stick to it. Cramming for exams takes on new meaning with a college workload. It's best to do a little at a time.

4. Study with a group. It helps to commiserate—especially about a tough subject.

5. Learn how to think analytically. College isn't about spewing out your teacher's opinions; you've got to form a few of your own too.

MYTH:

"I'm used to being in high school early, so getting up for an 8 A.M. class is no big deal, right?"

MYTHBUSTER:

Well . . . if there were an award for "class most likely skipped," the 8 A.M. class would win hands down. Remember, when you're away at college you don't have your parents telling you to go to bed (or to class). You might find yourself staying up until 2 A.M. studying or, more likely, having a deep convo with your roommate. Unless you are a super-perky morning person, you might want to choose classes that start a little later in the day.

99

You might get a little homesick at college—even if you couldn't **WAIT** to get out of town.

It's only natural to feel a little stressed about being away from family and friends for the first time.

What to do

1. Call your parents. They'll be glad to hear from you.
2. If you feel comfortable, talk to you roommate about it, or plan a fun activity together to help build the friendship.
3. Keep in touch with friends from home, but don't get upset if your best bud is having the time of his/her life. Everybody adjusts differently to a new environment.
4. Get involved in a club or activity. It's the best way to meet new people and to feel more comfortable on campus.

5. Research the Greek lifestyle on campus. If you decide to rush, and are accepted into a fraternity or sorority, you can enjoy a built-in support system to help you through college and a bunch of life-long friends!

6. Talk to your Resident Advisor (R.A.). He will be sympathetic and can probably help you get through homesickness as well as any stress or confusion you may be experiencing.

What not to do

1. Don't feel embarrassed about a tough adjustment.

2. Don't go straight to your room after class. Hang out in the quad, take a swim at the sports complex, etc.

3. Don't isolate yourself from making new friends. If someone asks if you want to grab a latte after class, say yes!

4. Don't wait to get help if your transition blues seem to get worse as the semester progresses. If you can't shake the blues after talking to your R.A., go to the counseling center, or seek out the advice of a spiritual leader. You are not alone—there are plenty of people trained to help you through the rough patches!

You're not going to be perfect—and nobody expects you to be.

College is a challenge for most students—a challenge you must conquer all by yourself. Don't be surprised if you don't get a 4.0 the first semester.

Sensory overload

It's no big shocker—there's a lot happening on campus.

- tough professors
- loads of homework and exams
- living with roommates and making new friends
- going on dates
- interesting activities and clubs
- parties
- freedom!

Balancing act: party vs. performance

1. Remember why you're in college. To get an education.

2. Parrr-taaay without guilt. Budget time in order of importance: classes, studying/homework, other responsibilities (like a job), extracurricular activities, free time/F-U-N!

3. Assess your study habits. Working your butt off and still getting poor grades? Maybe your high school habits need an upgrade. Join a study group and ask your academic advisor for suggestions too. Your grades won't improve overnight, so be patient.

101

Find your dream.
Find your passion.
Find YOURSELF!

You are about to embark on the most awesome, exciting, and wonderfully exhilarating time of your life. Don't waste it by just going with the flow. Use it to find out what makes you tick . . . and what makes you happy.

Go for it!

Come on! It's the perfect time to explore the world and take a few risks. Use it or lose it!

____ *Choose a few "different" classes in addition to your core curriculum such as folklore, acting, or Judo.*

____ *Make friends with people who are NOT like you.*

____ *Study abroad for a semester. When else are you going to have time to experience life in a foreign country?*

____ *Become politically active—you're a voter now!*

____ *Experience the country's diversity; take lots of road trips!*

____ *Try internships in several fields of business.*

____ *Open your mind to new ideas and different opinions— become a critical thinker!*

____ *Go to theatre productions, on and off campus.*

____ *Explore your surroundings, whether it be downtown Chicago or the hills of Vermont.*